TUSCANY 360°

Photographs by Ghigo Roli
Sketches by Luisa Romussi

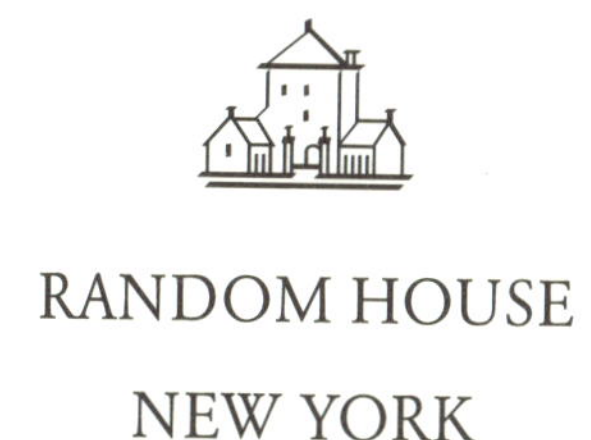

RANDOM HOUSE
NEW YORK

Published in the United States by Random House, Inc., New York, and simultaneously in Canada by Random House of Canada Limited, Toronto.

Library of Congress Cataloging-in-Publication Data

Roli, Ghigo
Tuscany 360° / photographs by Ghigo Roli, sketches by Luisa Romussi–
1st American ed.
p. cm.
ISBN 0-375-50410-9
1. Tuscany (Italy)–Pictorial works. 2. Photography, Panoramic.
I. Title: Tuscany three hundred sixty degrees. II. Romussi, Luisa. III. Title.
DG734.4.R67 2000
914.5′5′00222–dc21 99-044106

Random House website address: www.atrandom.com

Printed in Italy by Mariogros, Turin

24689753

FIRST AMERICAN EDITION

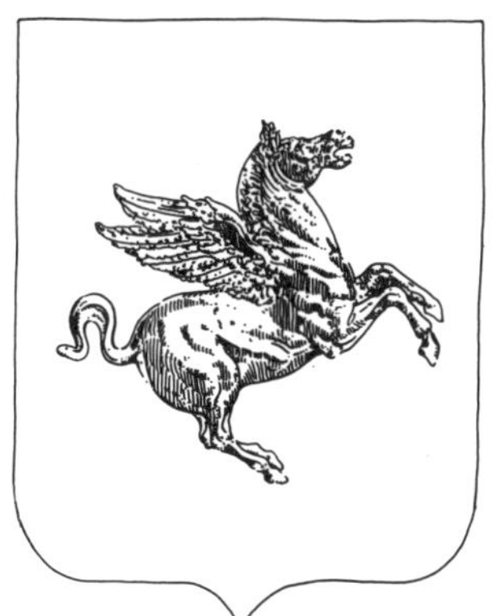

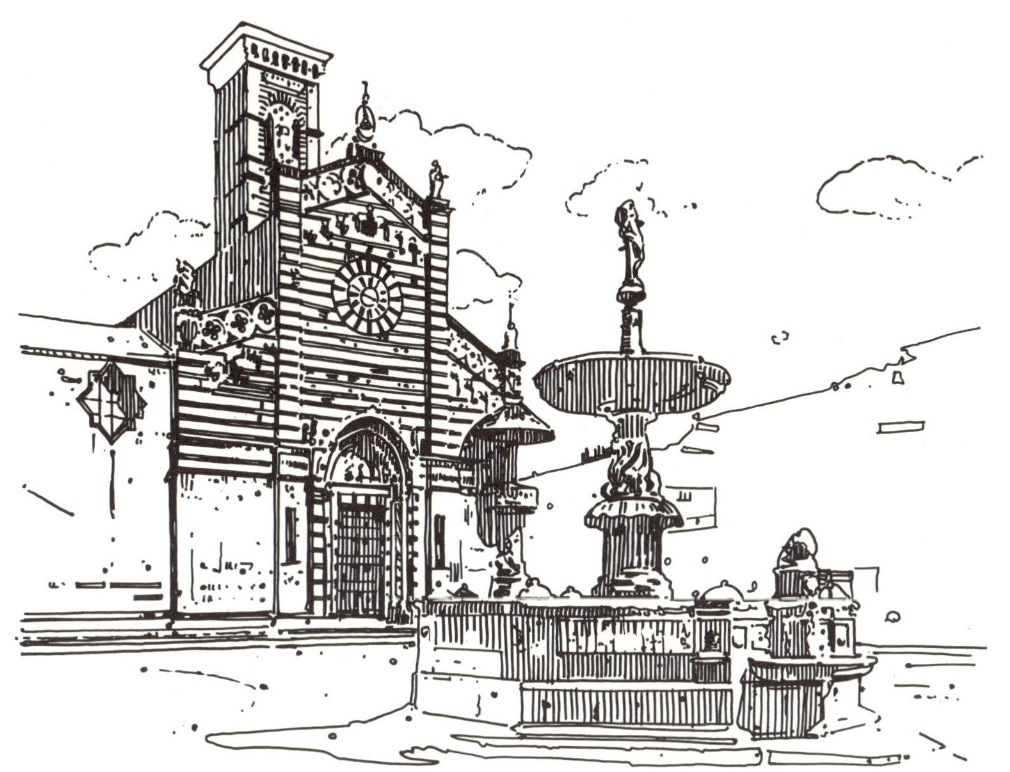

1.

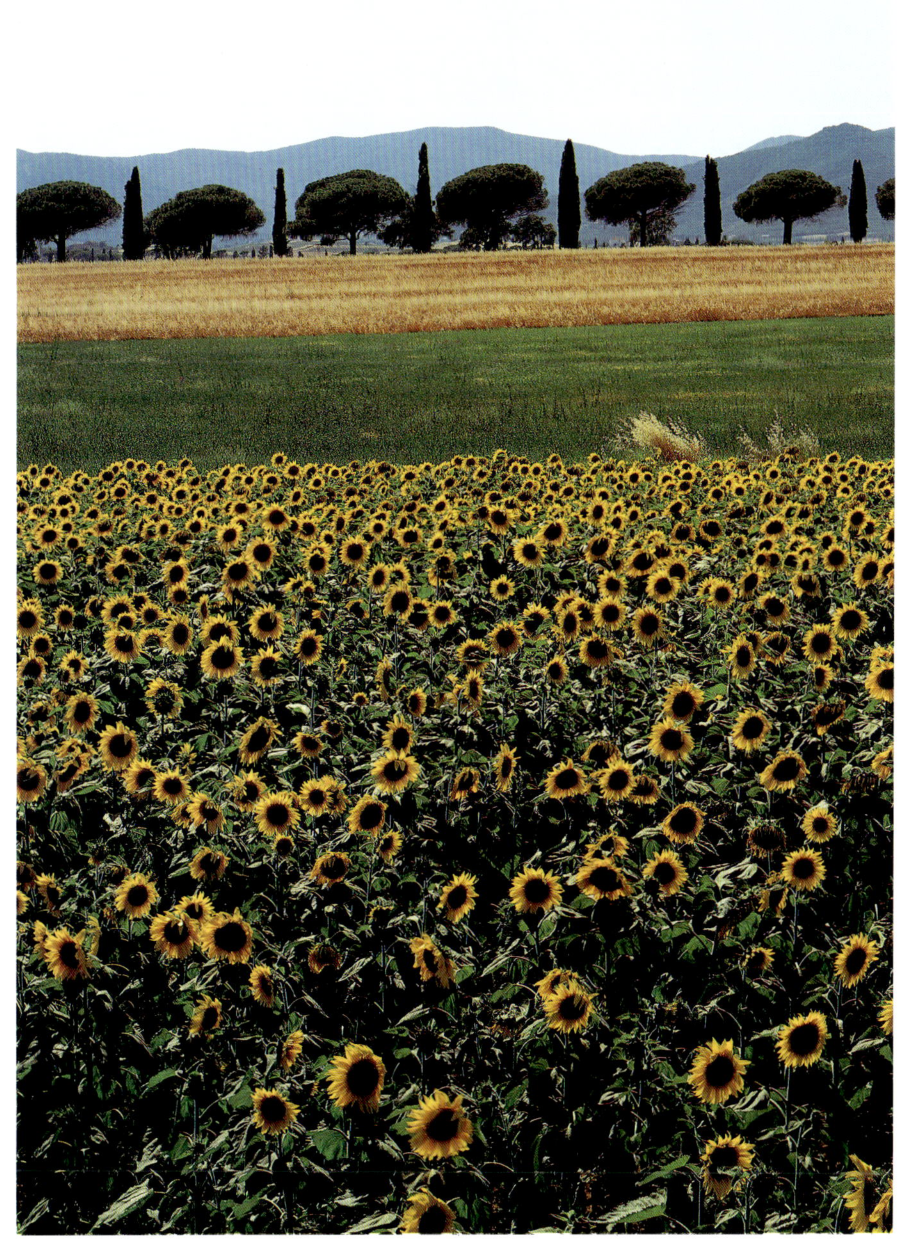

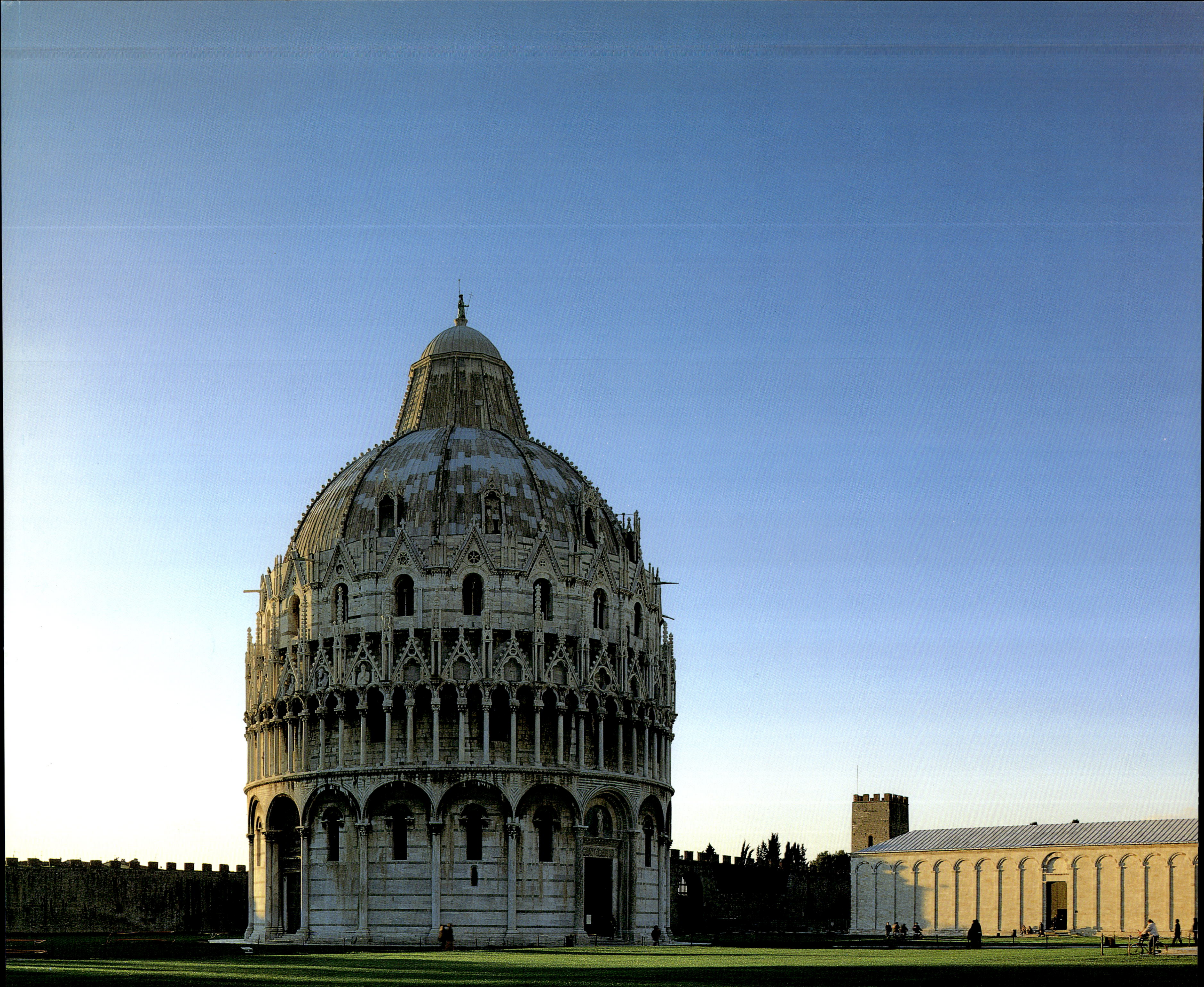

◄2. 3.

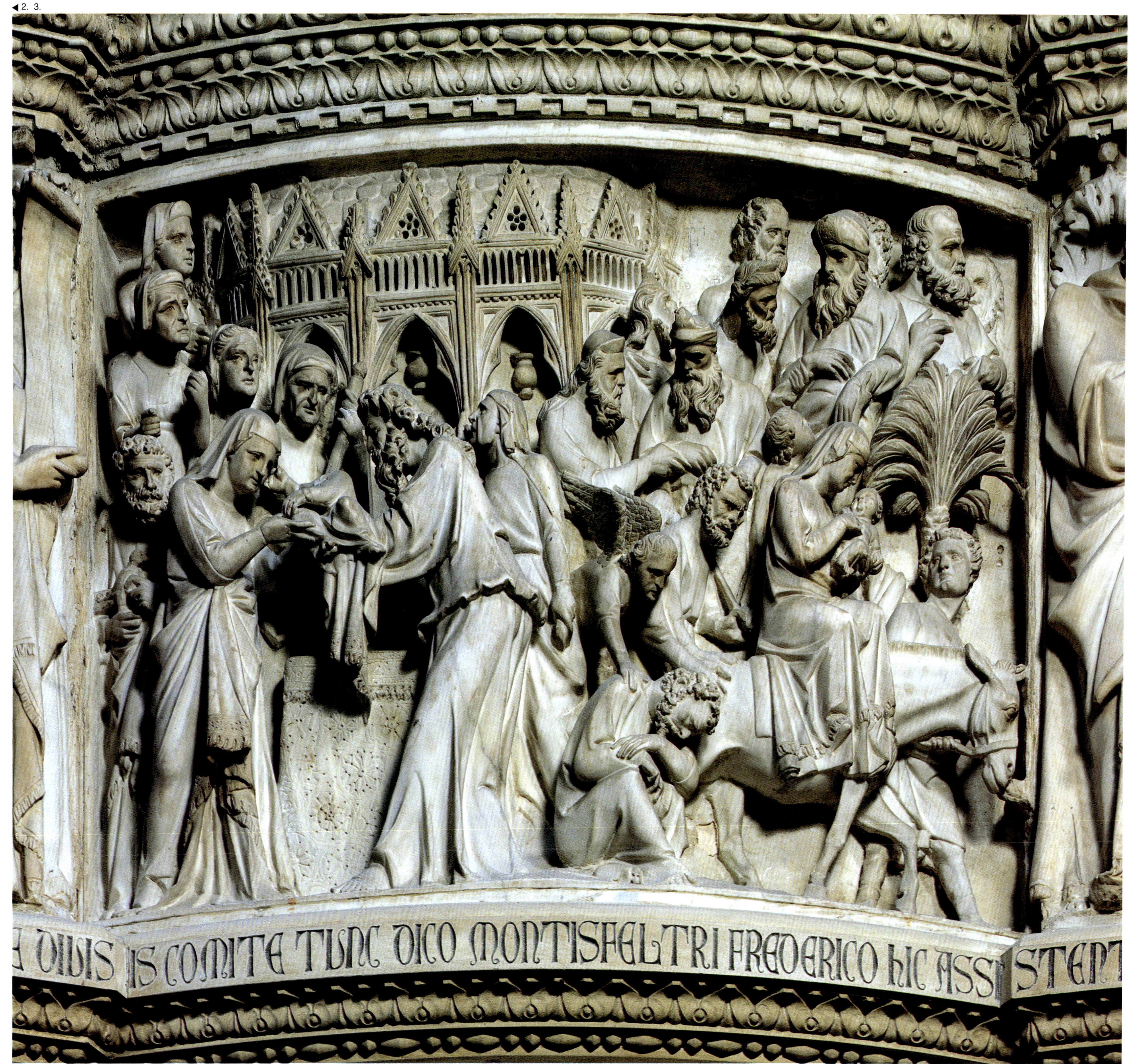
DIVIS
IS COMITE TUNC DICO MONTISFELTRI FREDERICO HIC ASSI
STENT

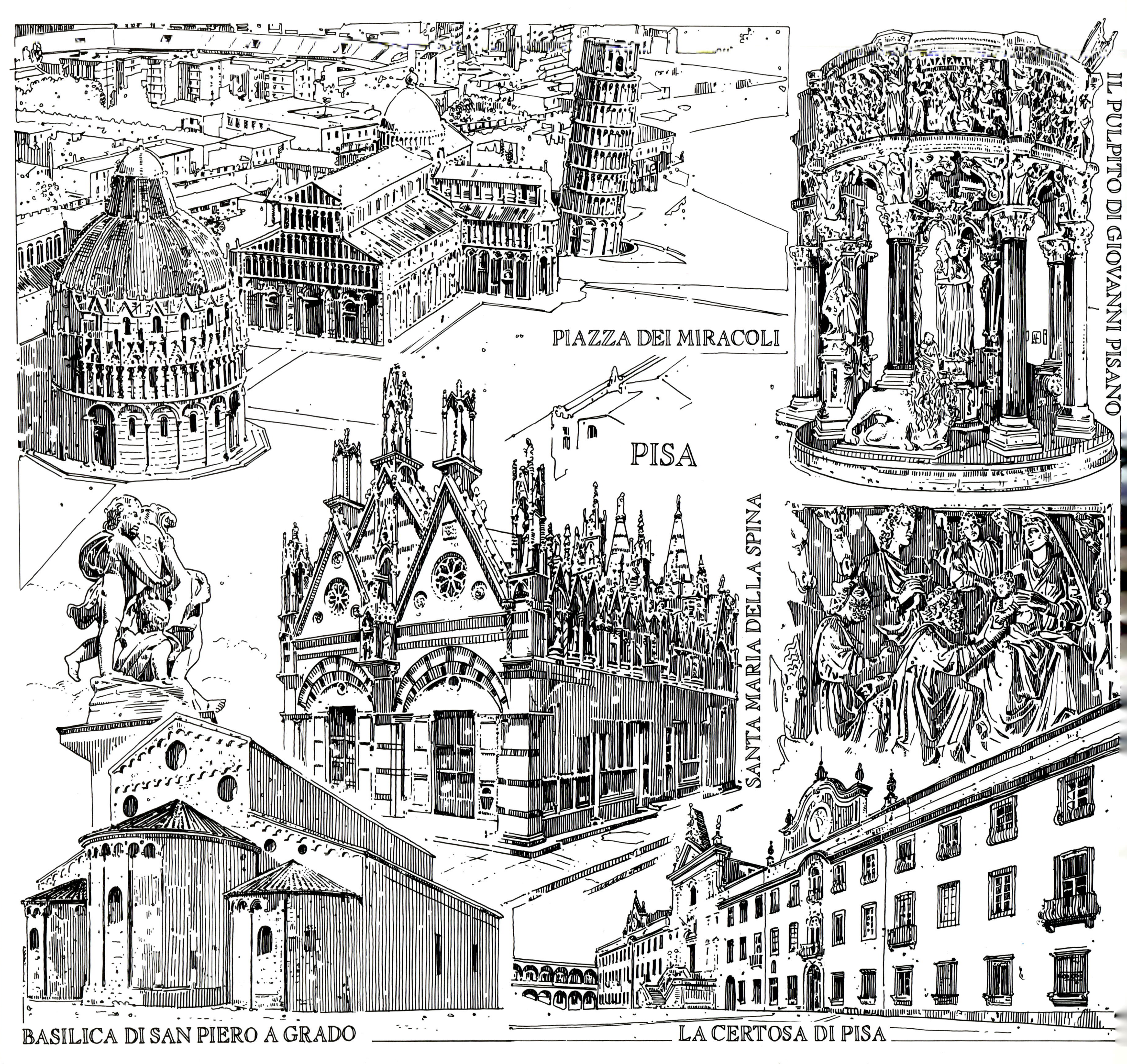
PIAZZA DEI MIRACOLI
IL PULPITO DI GIOVANNI PISANO
PISA
SANTA MARIA DELLA SPINA
BASILICA DI SAN PIERO A GRADO
LA CERTOSA DI PISA

4.

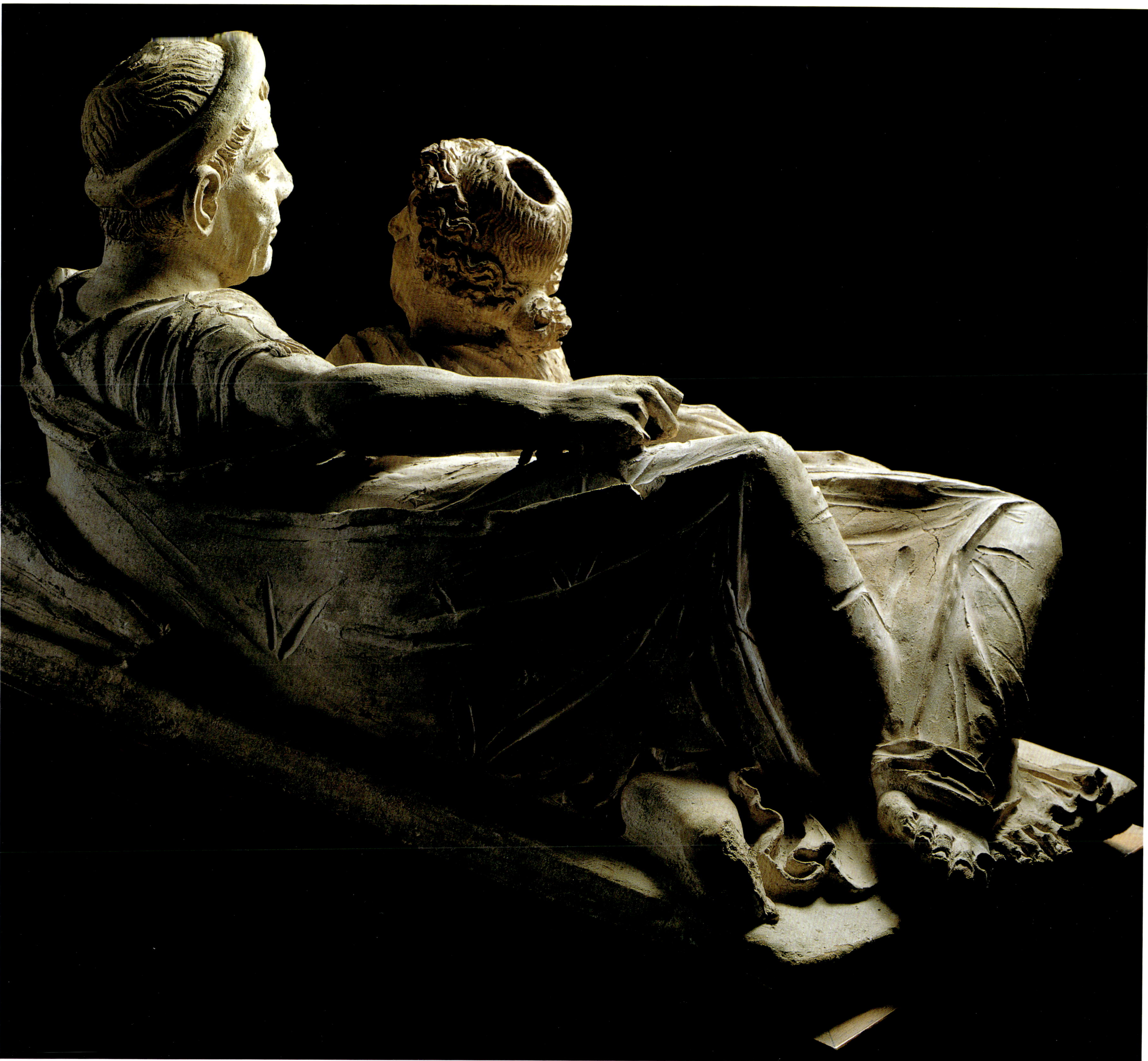

5.

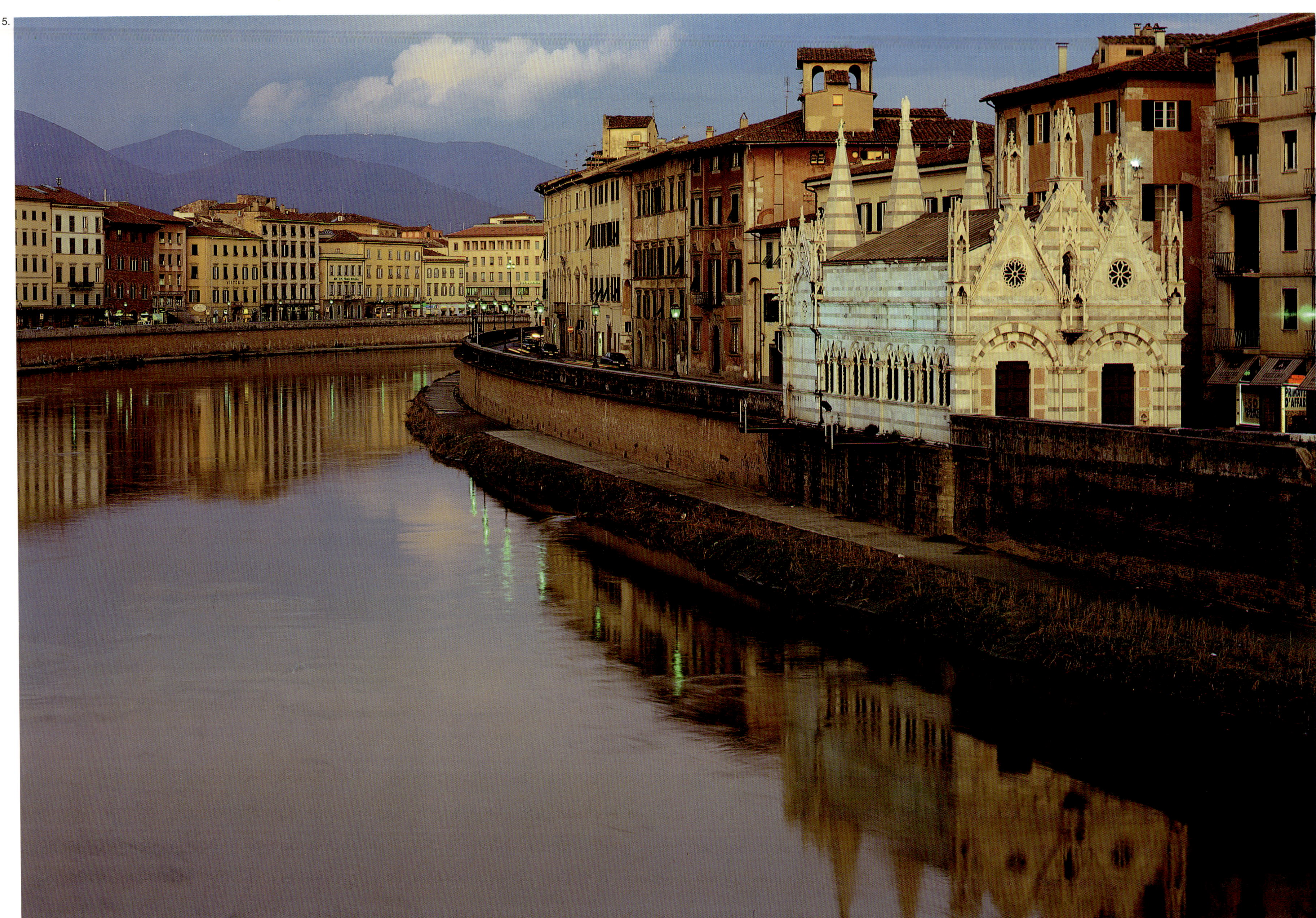

6.

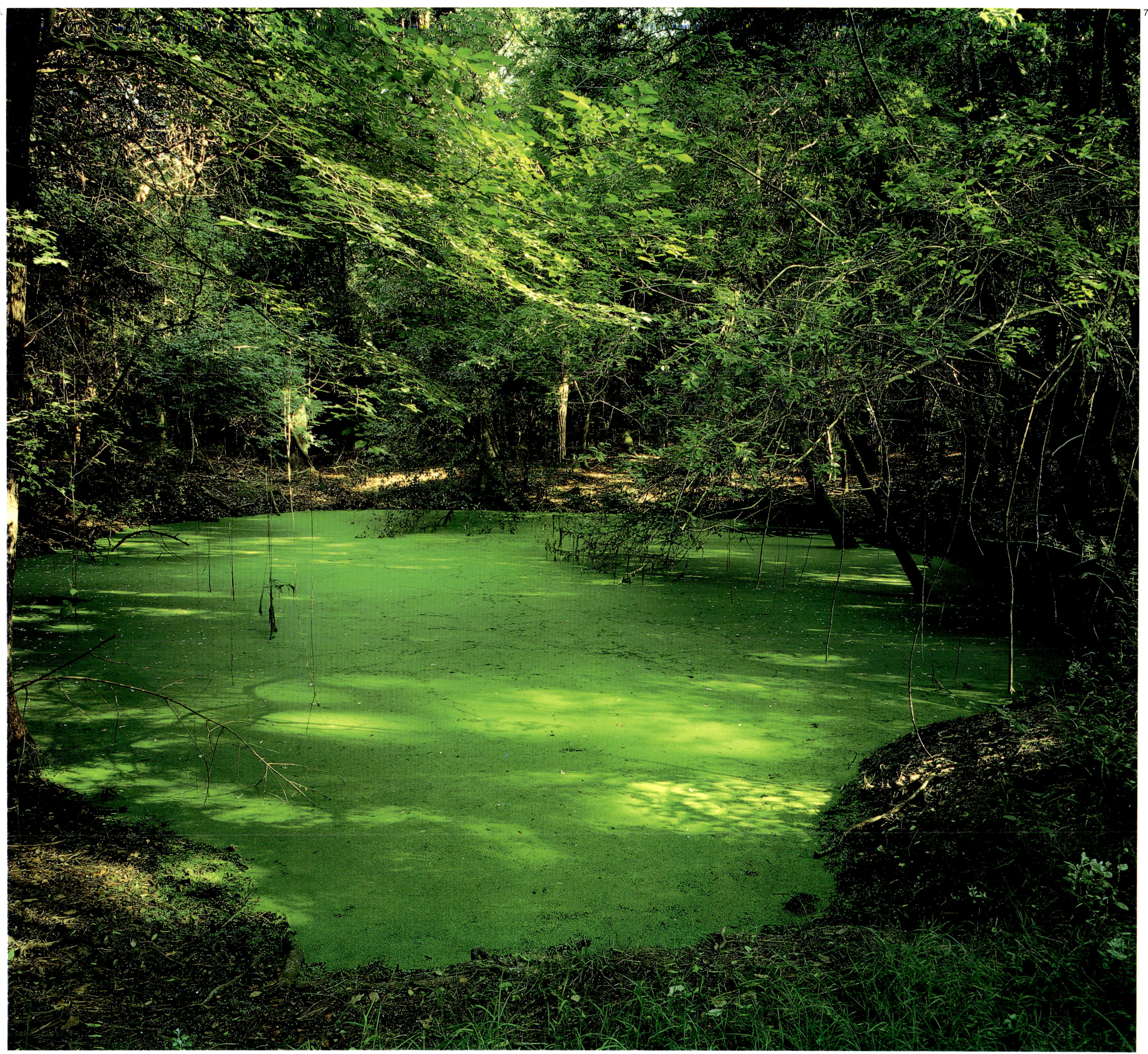

7. ▶

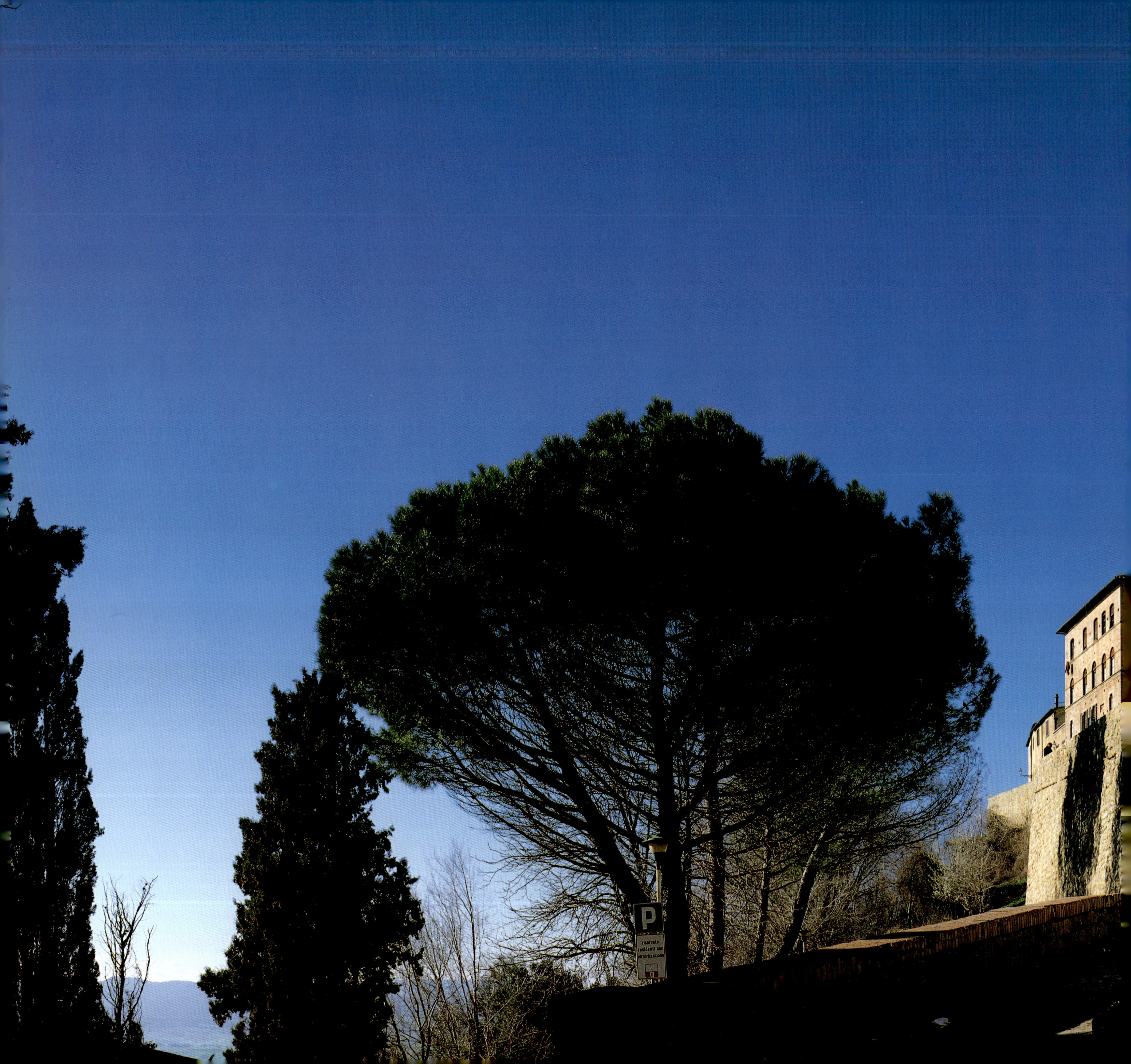
P
riservato
residenti con
autorizzazione

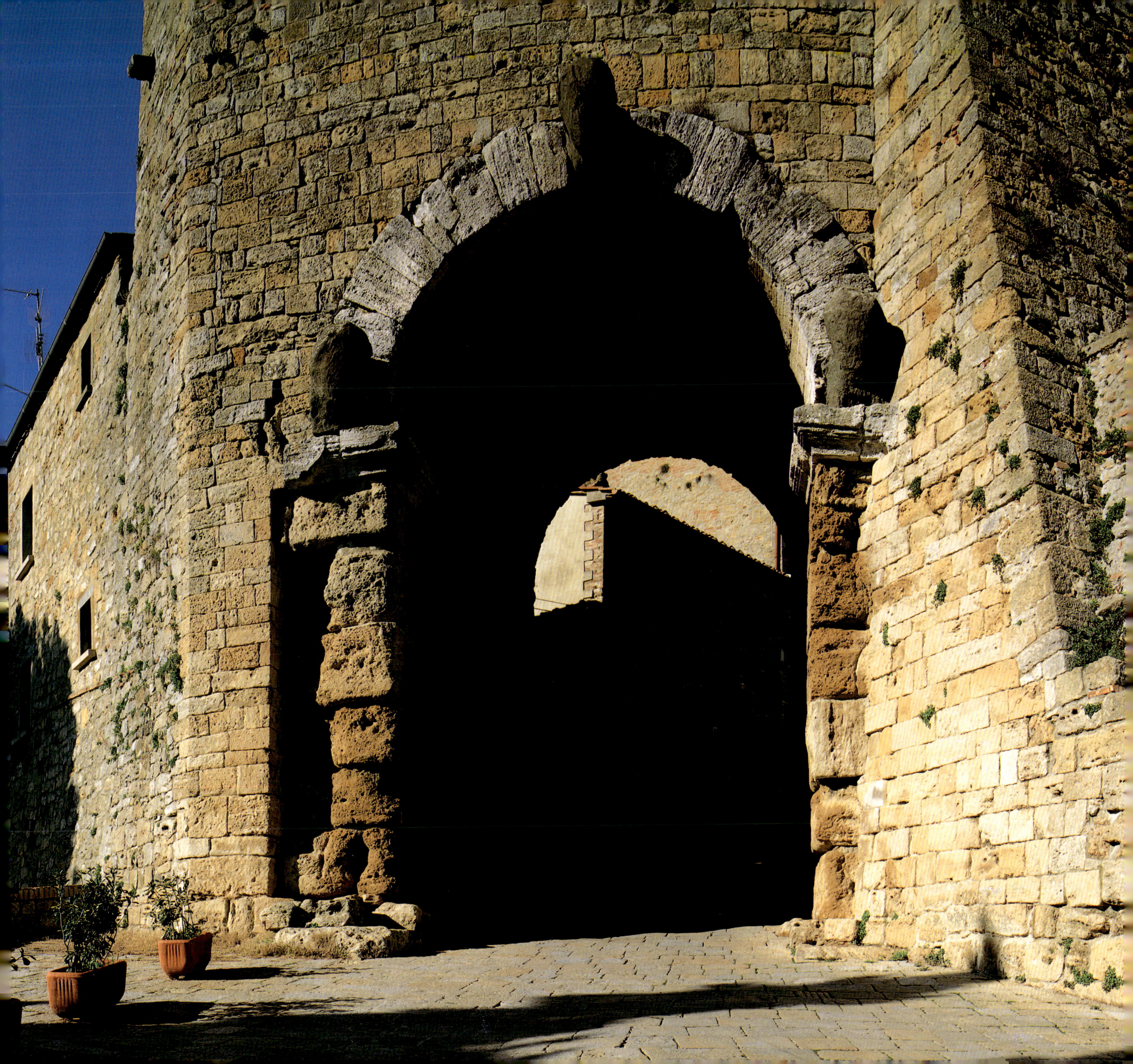

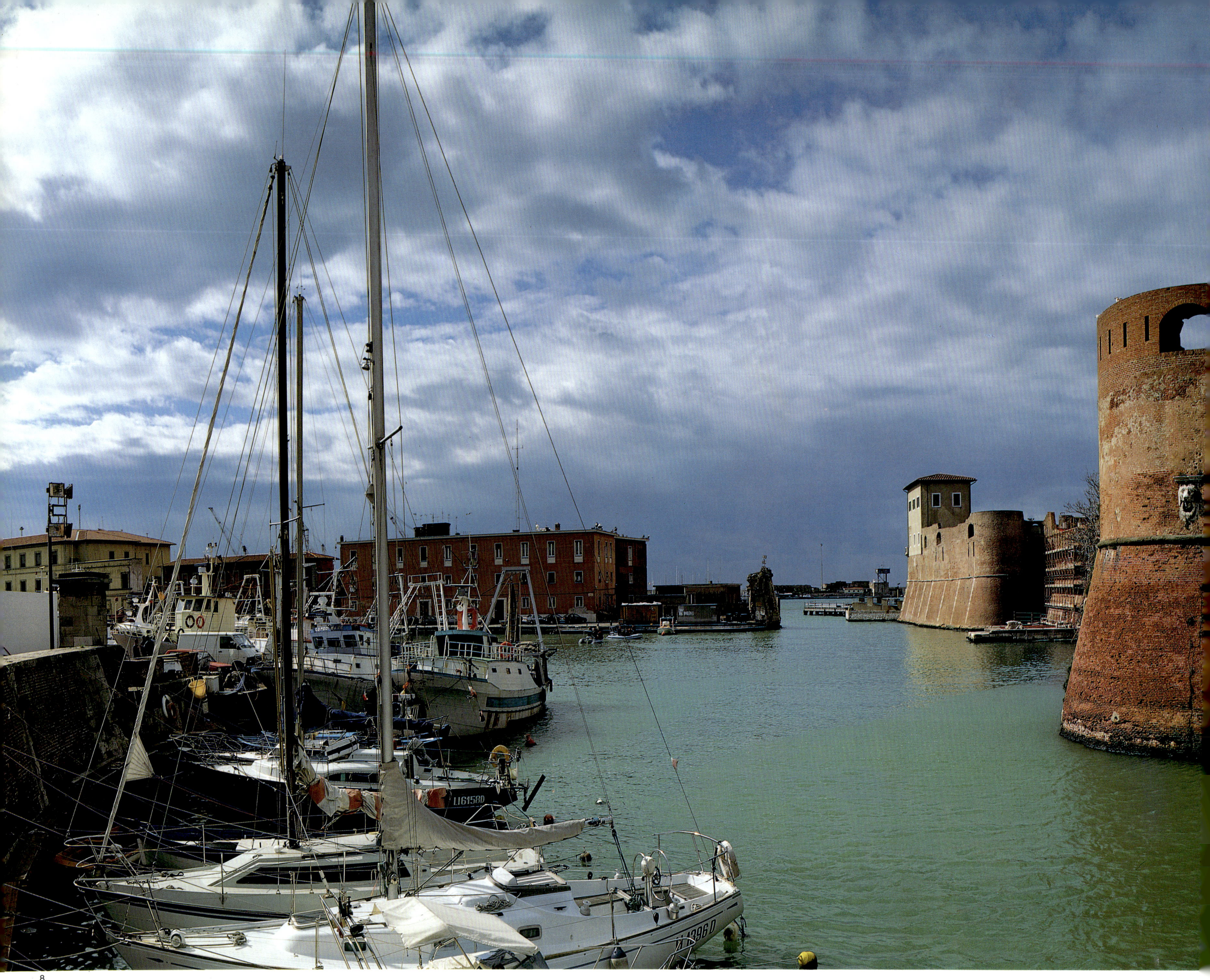

8.

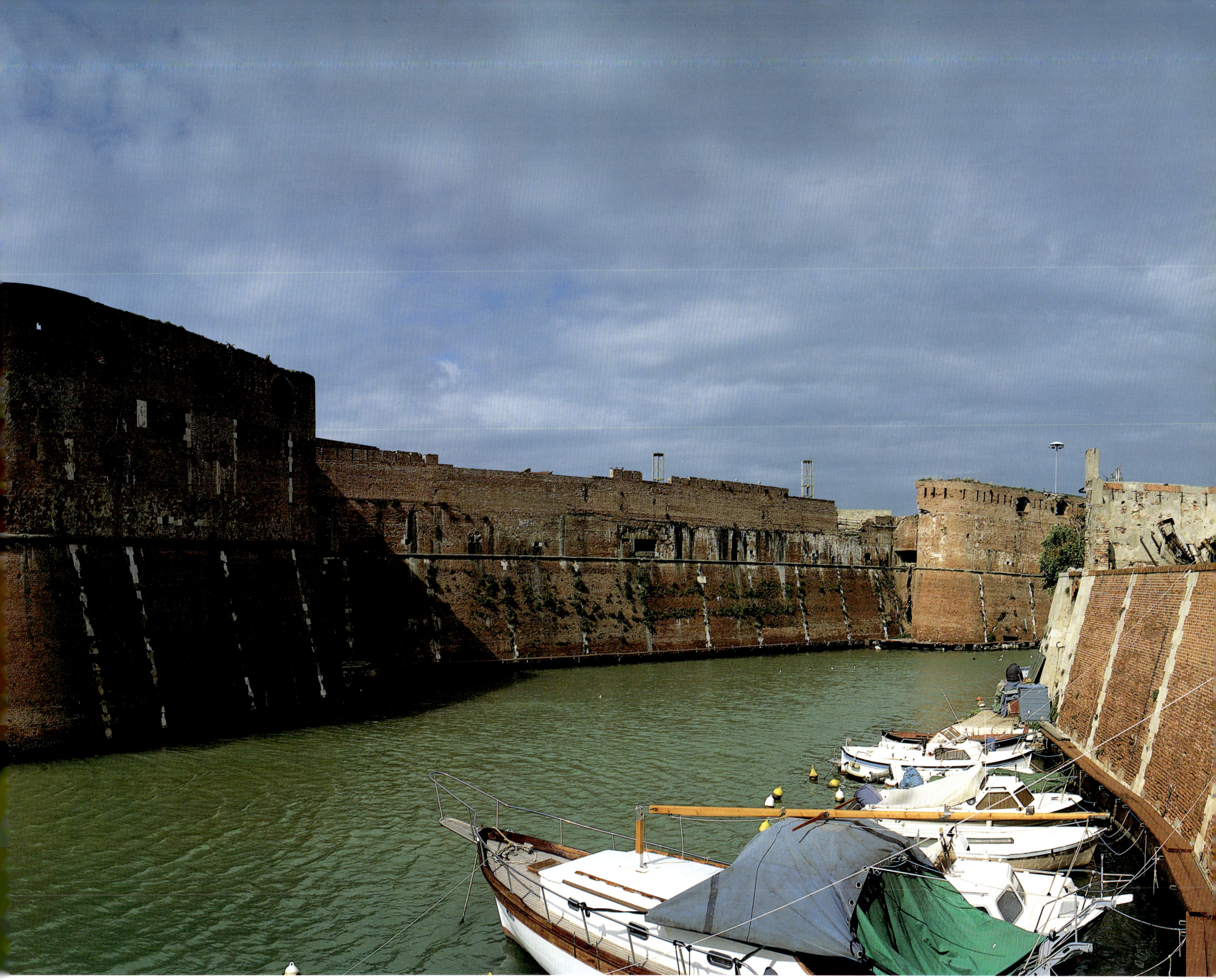

9.

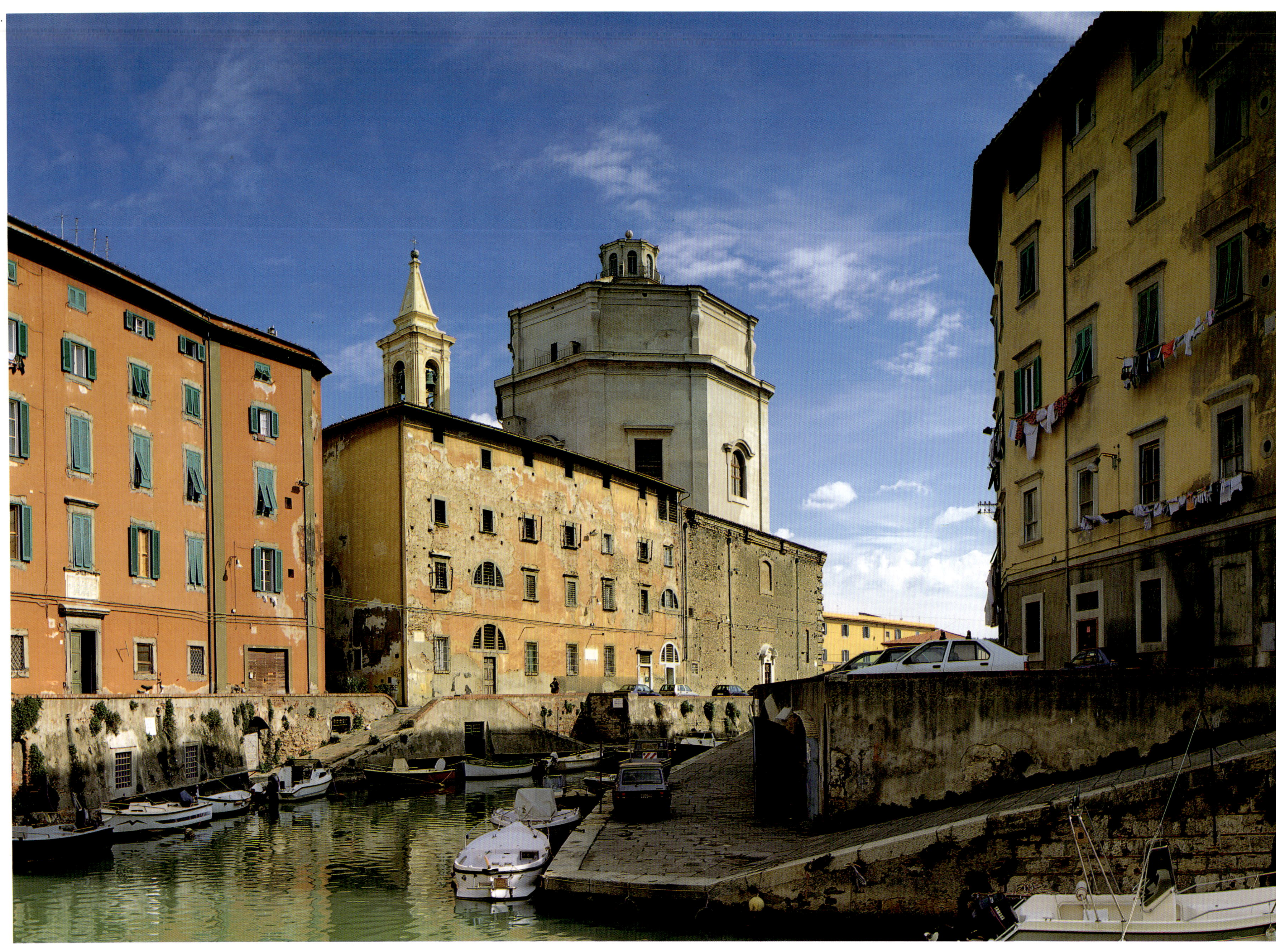

10.

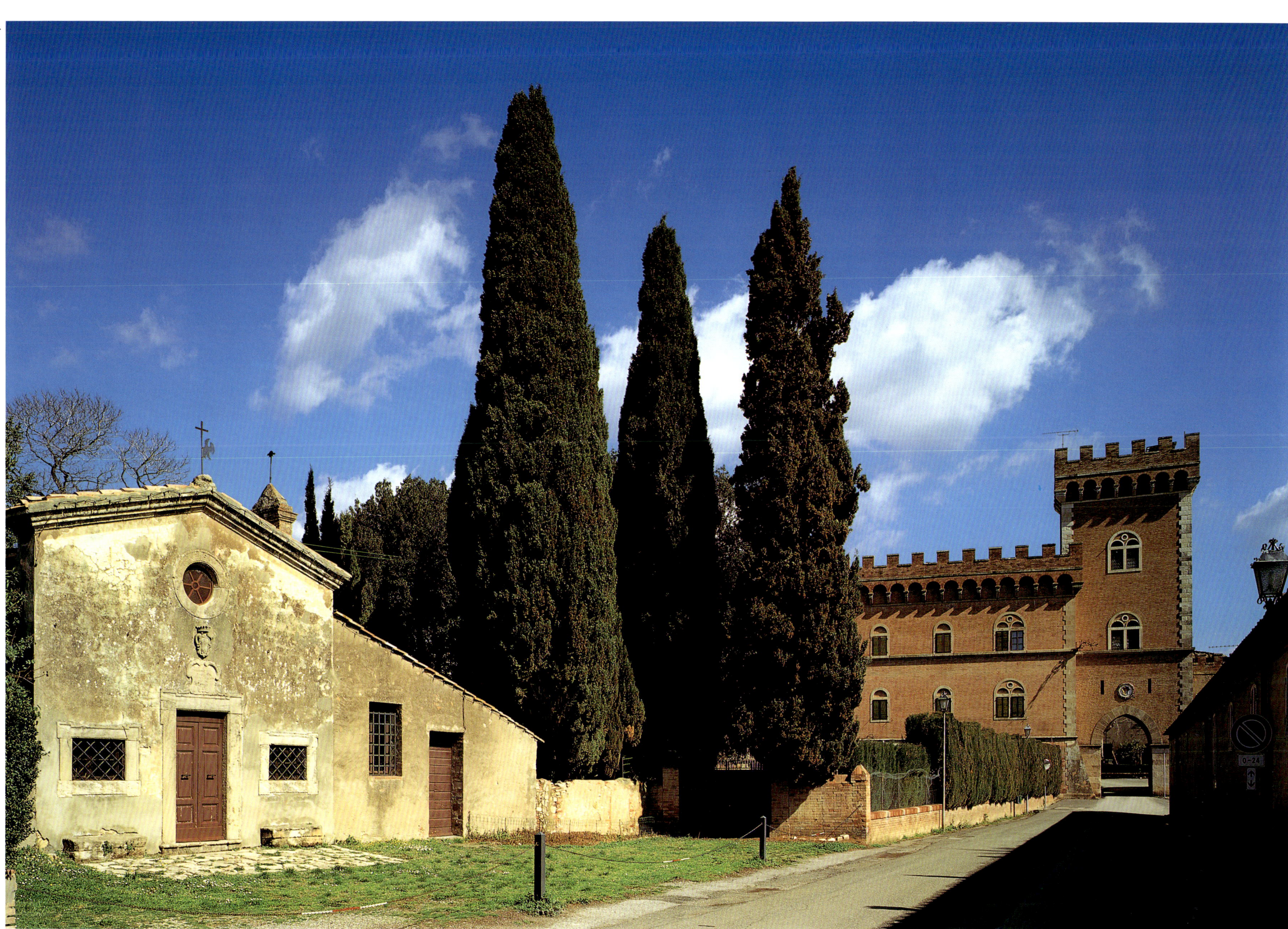

11.

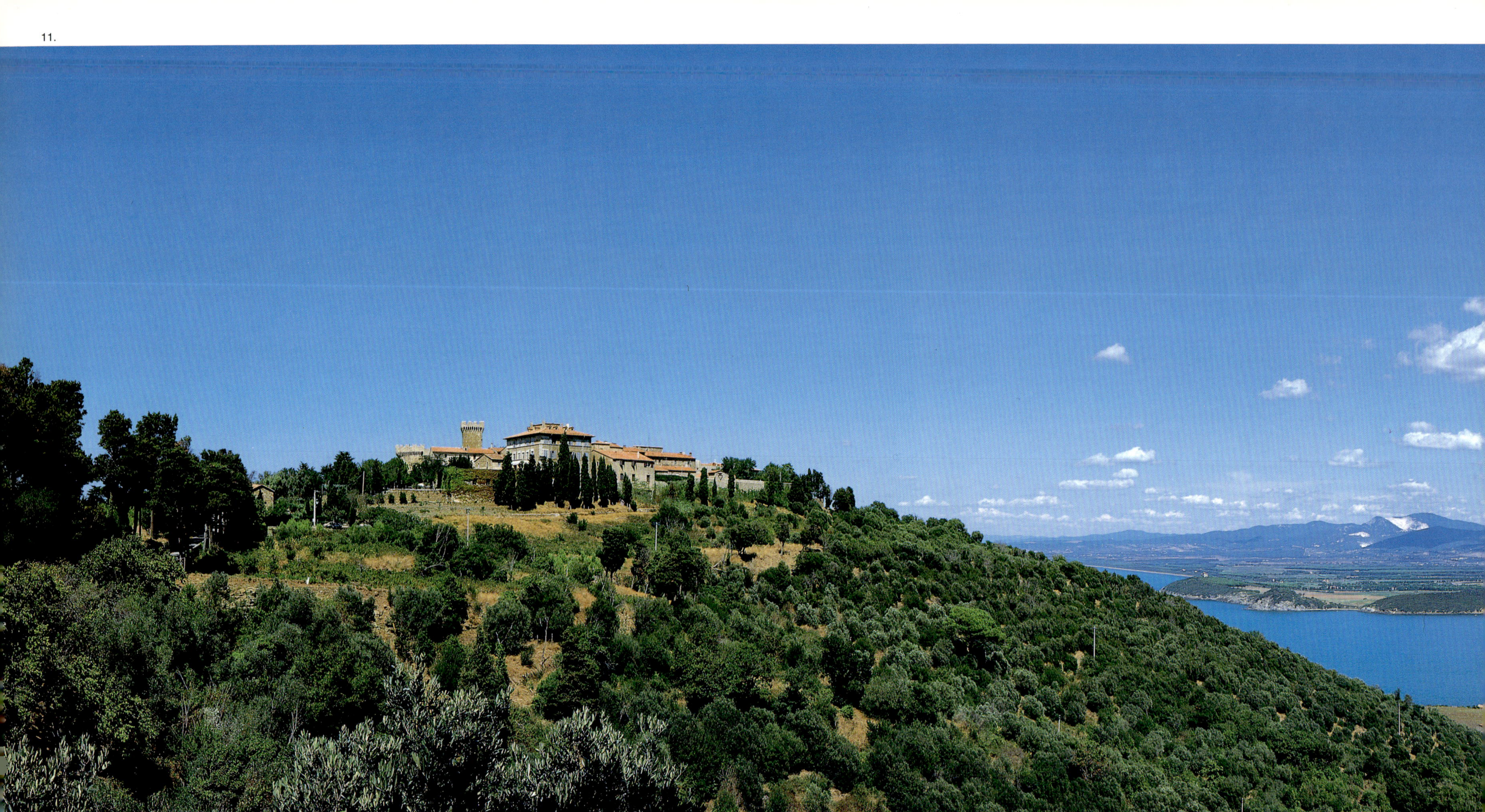

12. ▶

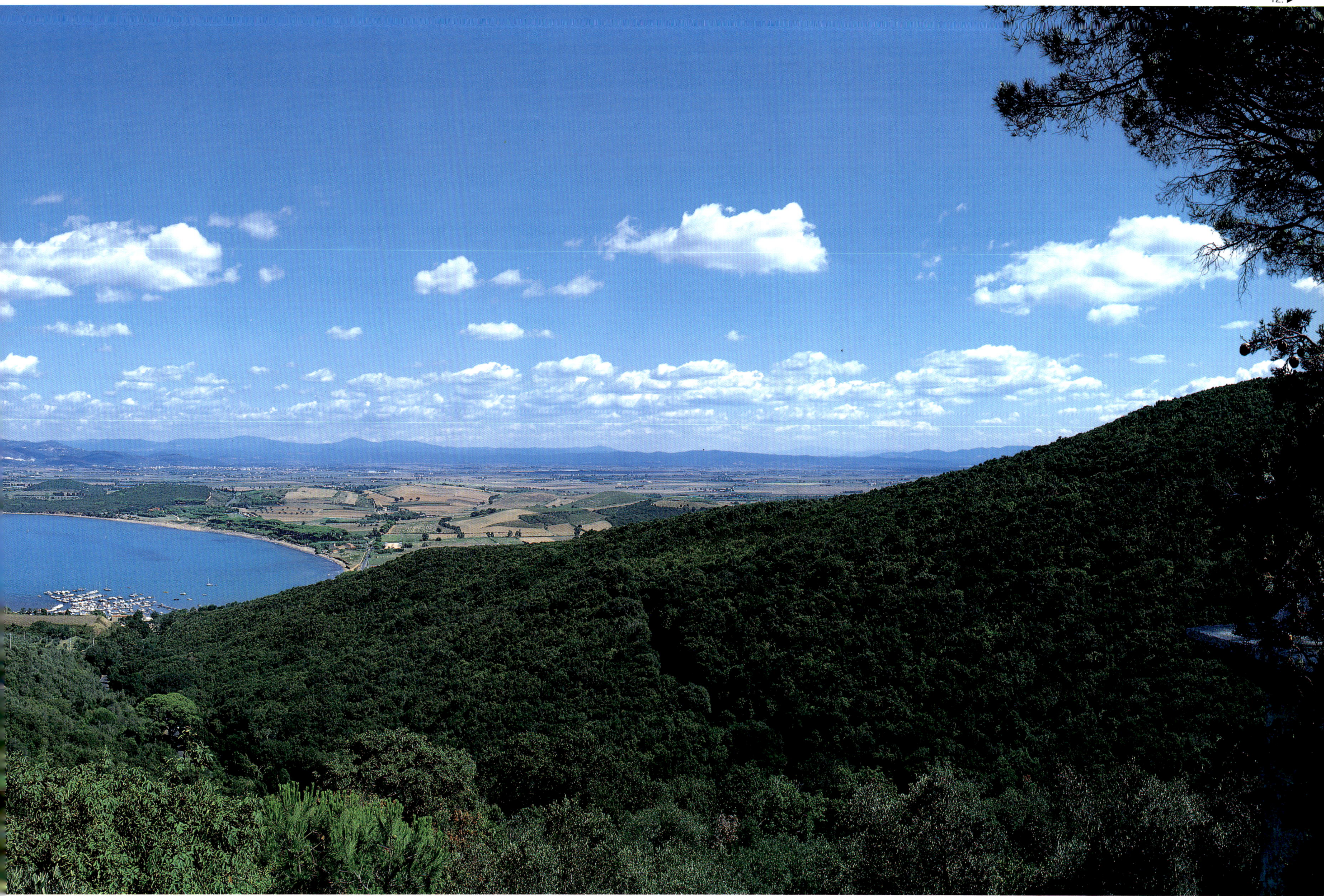

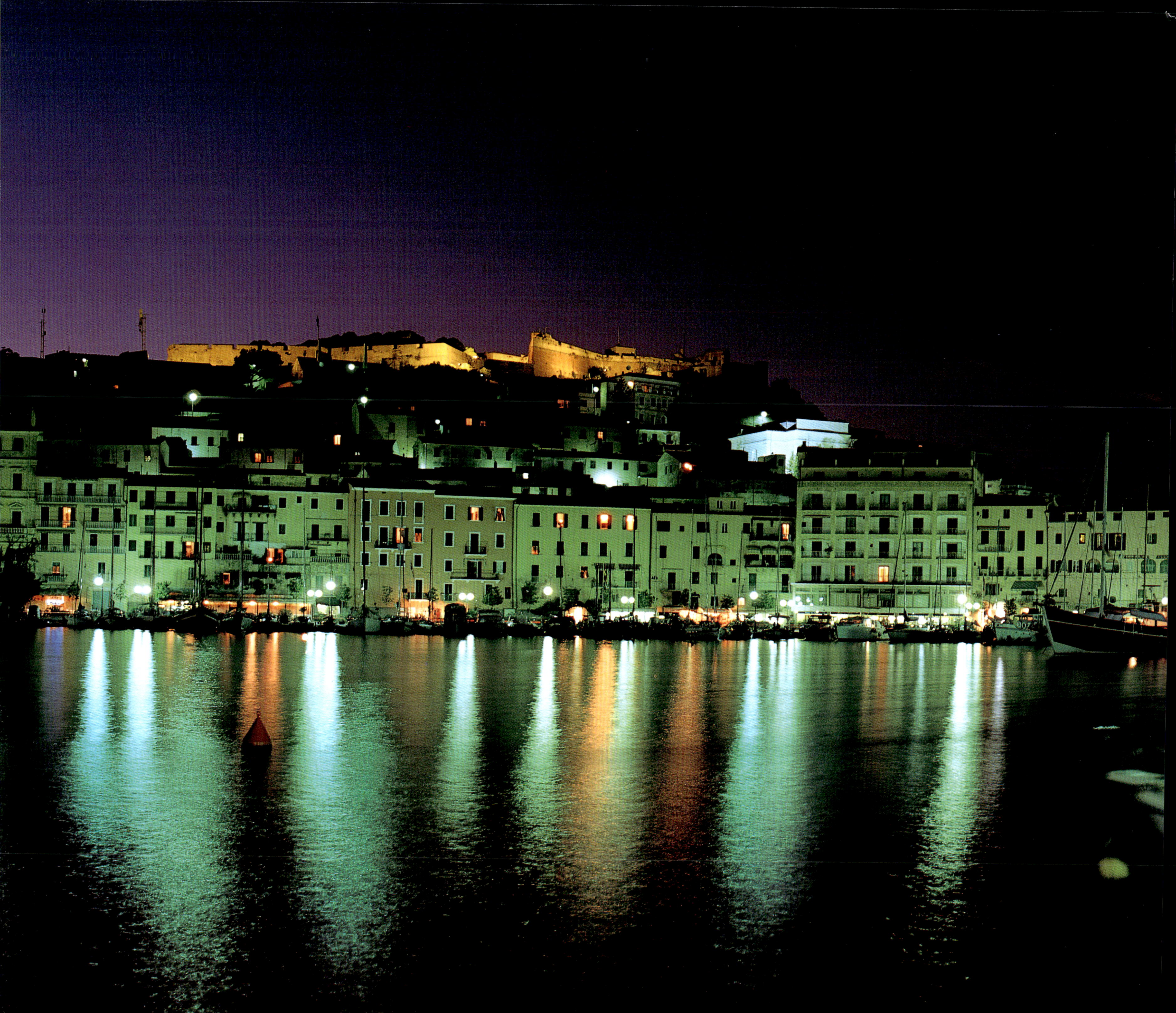

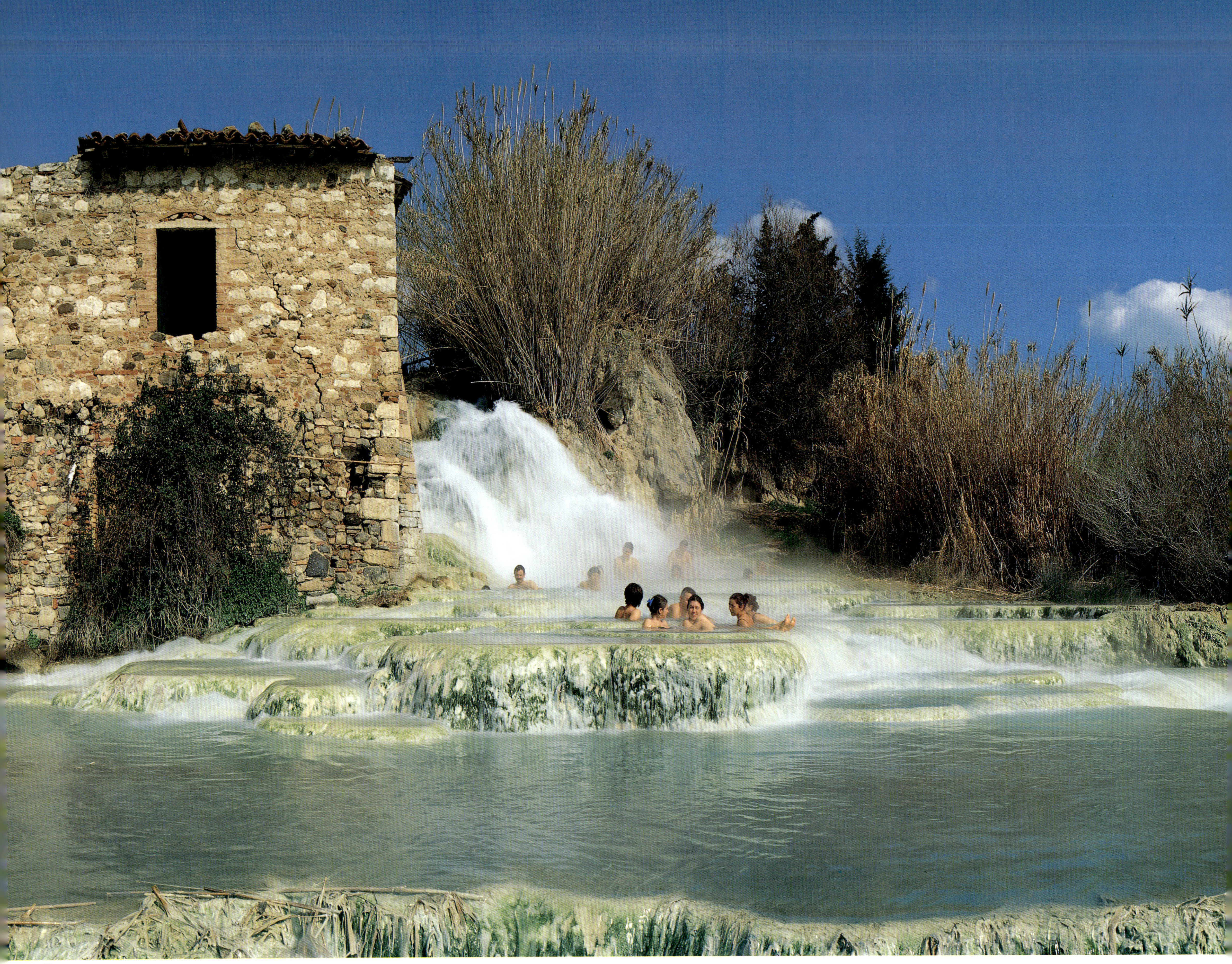

13.

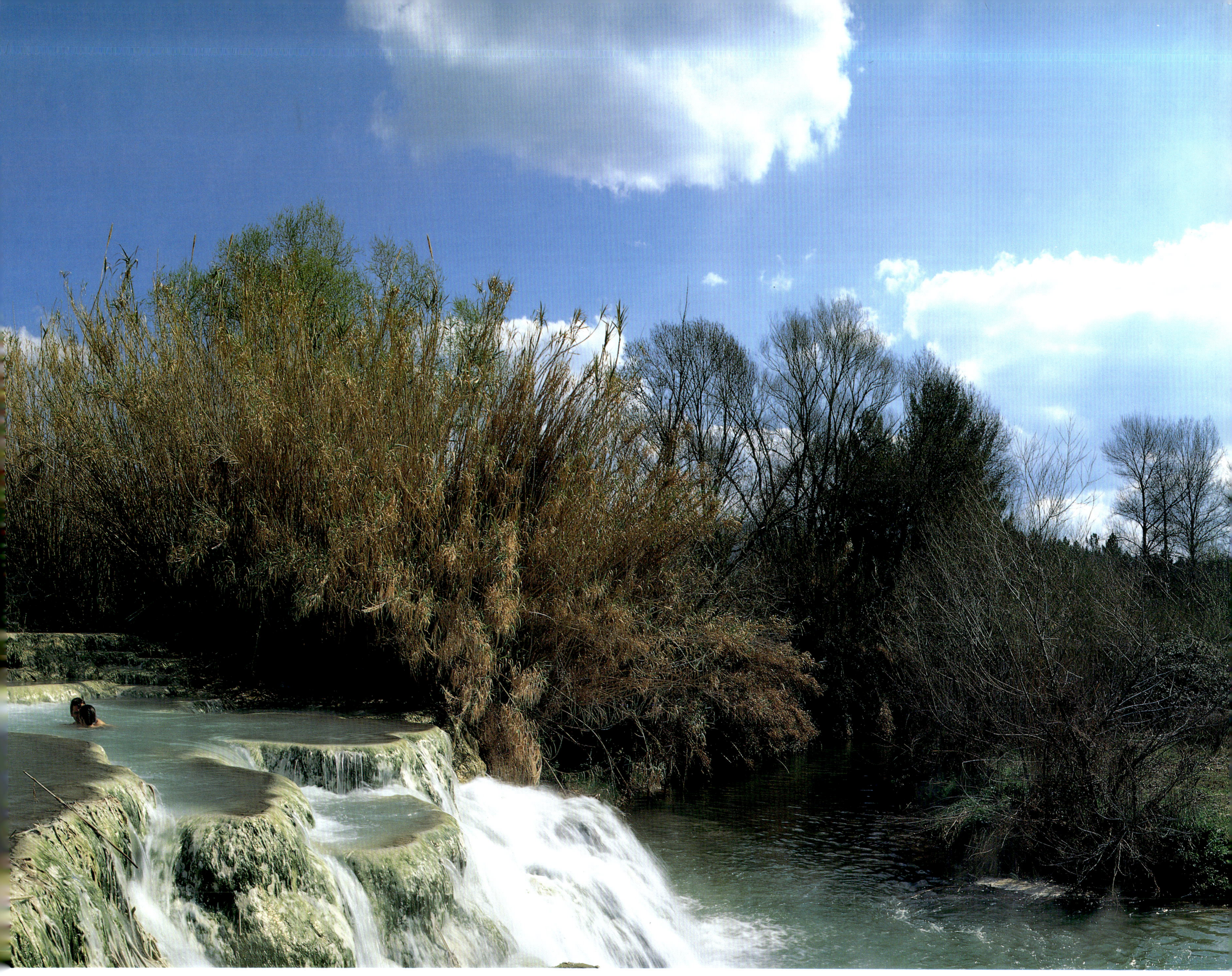

14.

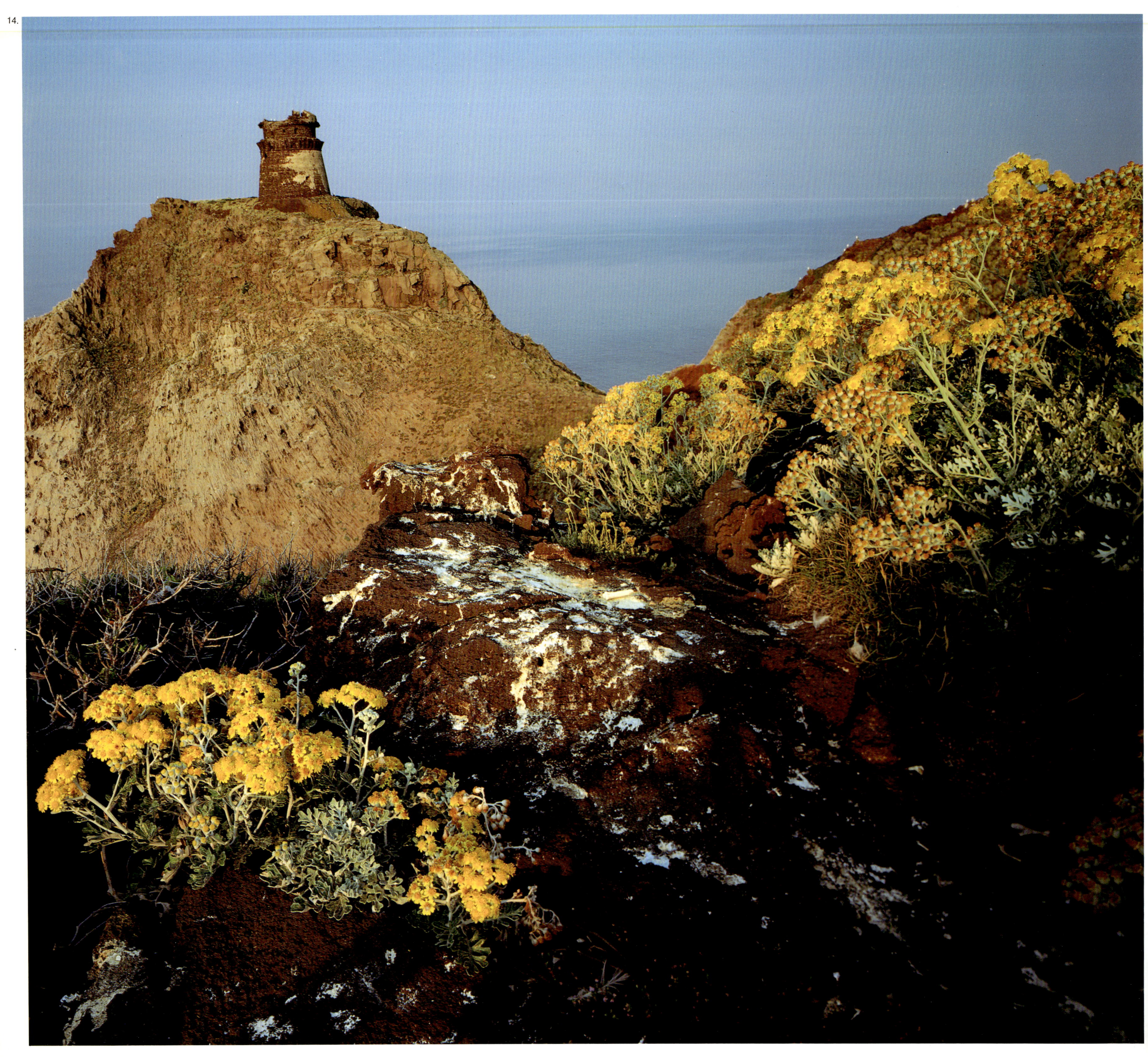

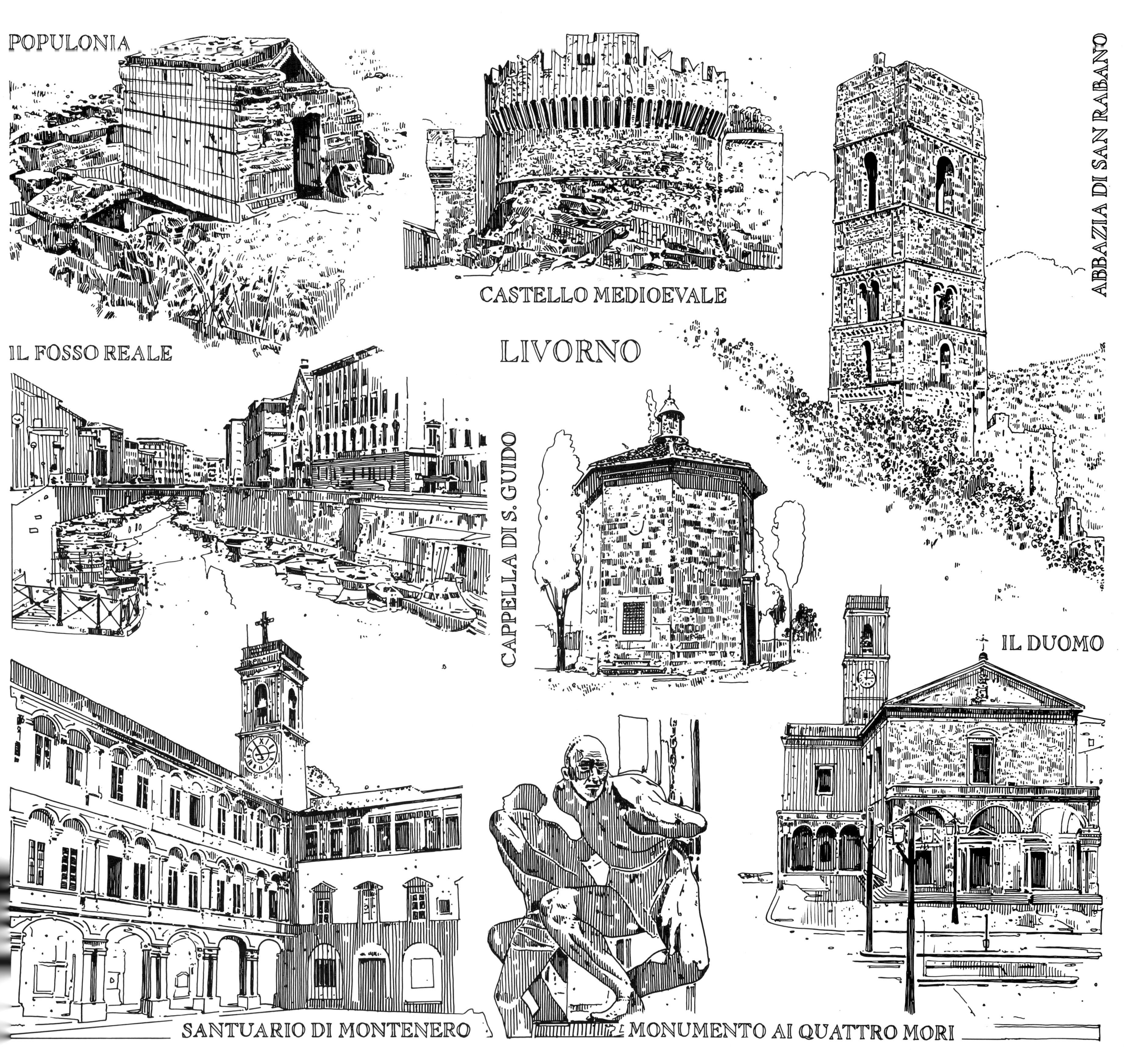
POPULONIA
CASTELLO MEDIOEVALE
ABBAZIA DI SAN RABANO
IL FOSSO REALE
LIVORNO
CAPPELLA DI S. GUIDO
IL DUOMO
SANTUARIO DI MONTENERO
MONUMENTO AI QUATTRO MORI

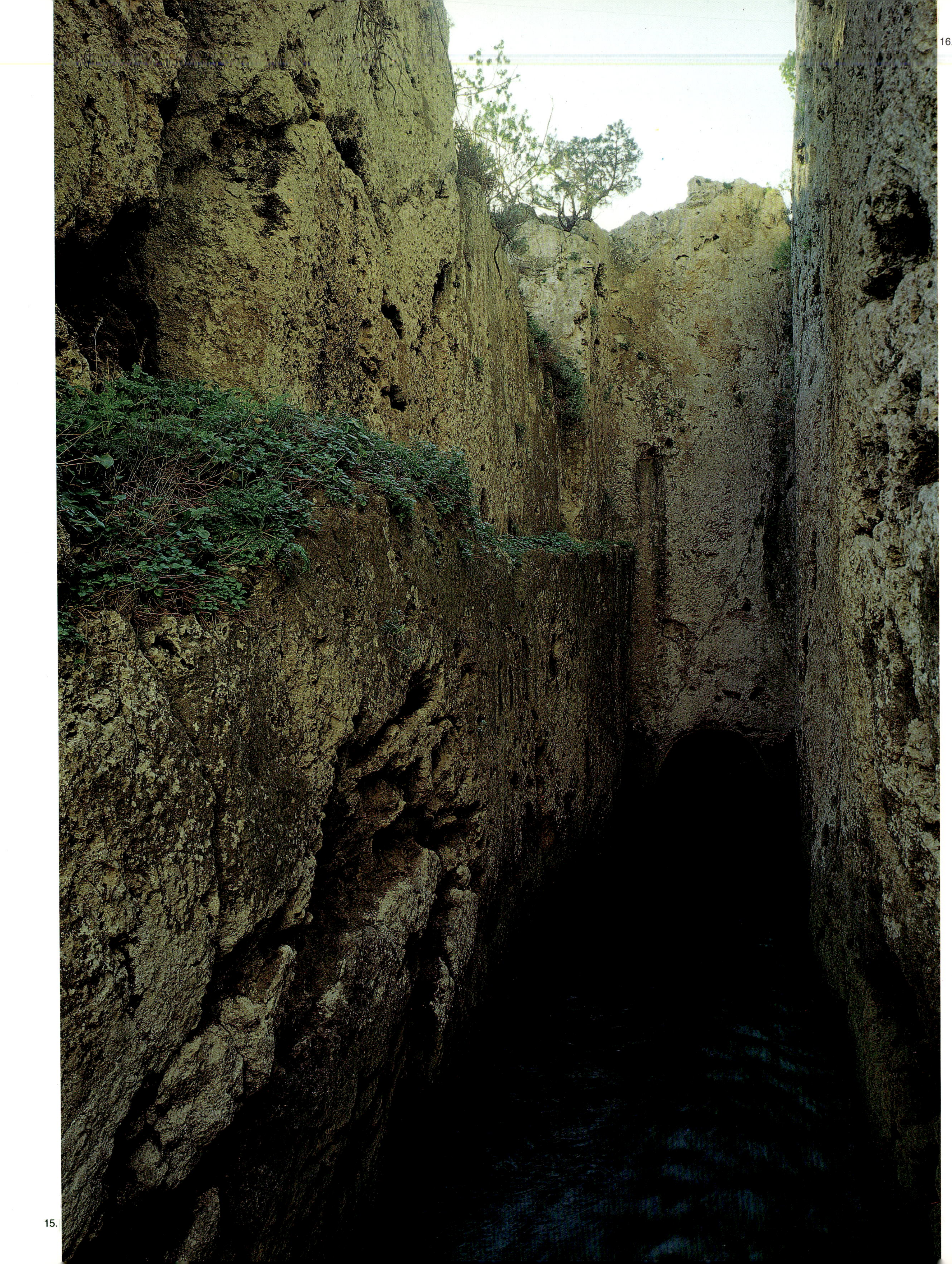

15.

16. ▶

17

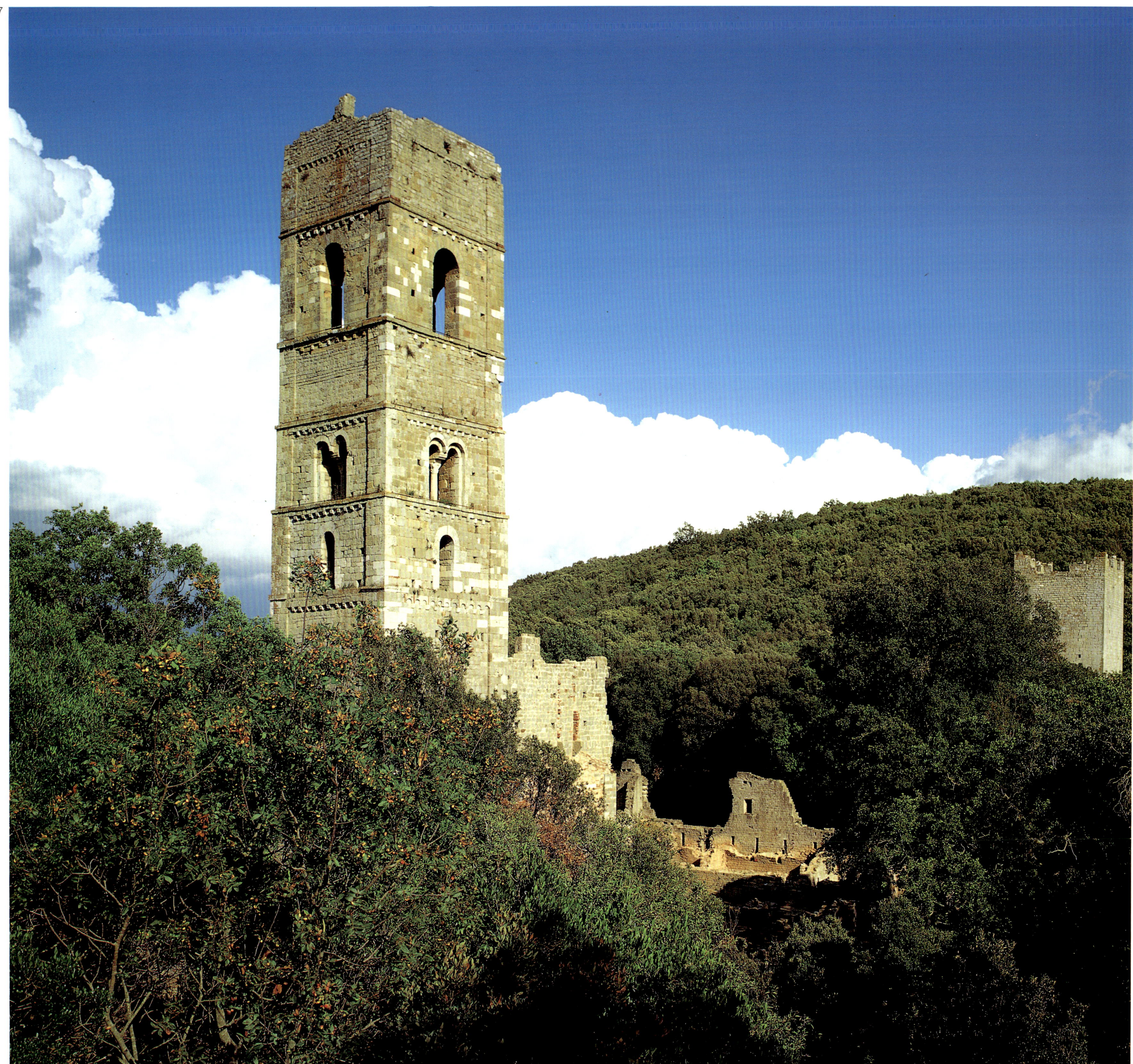

18.

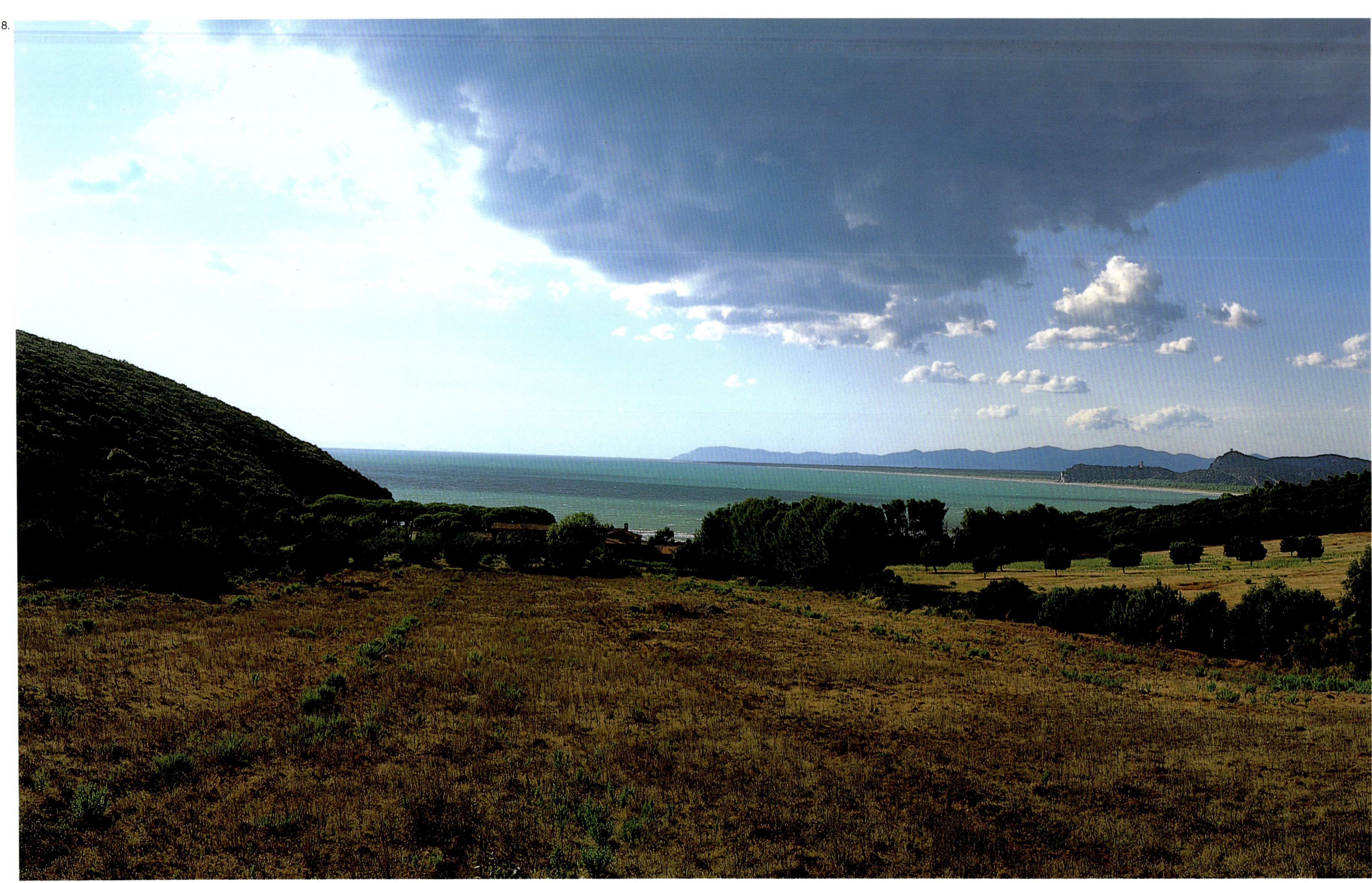

19.

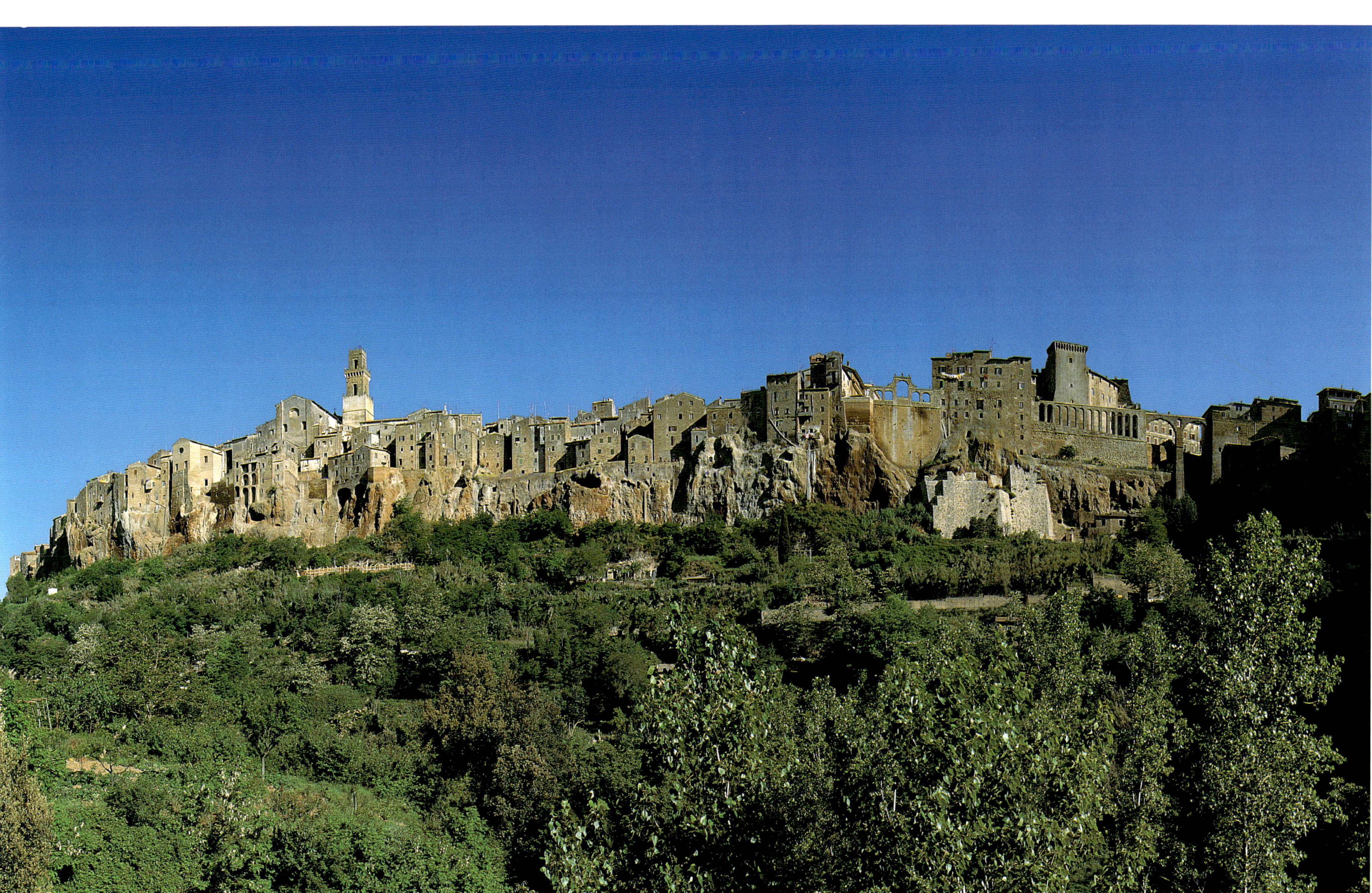

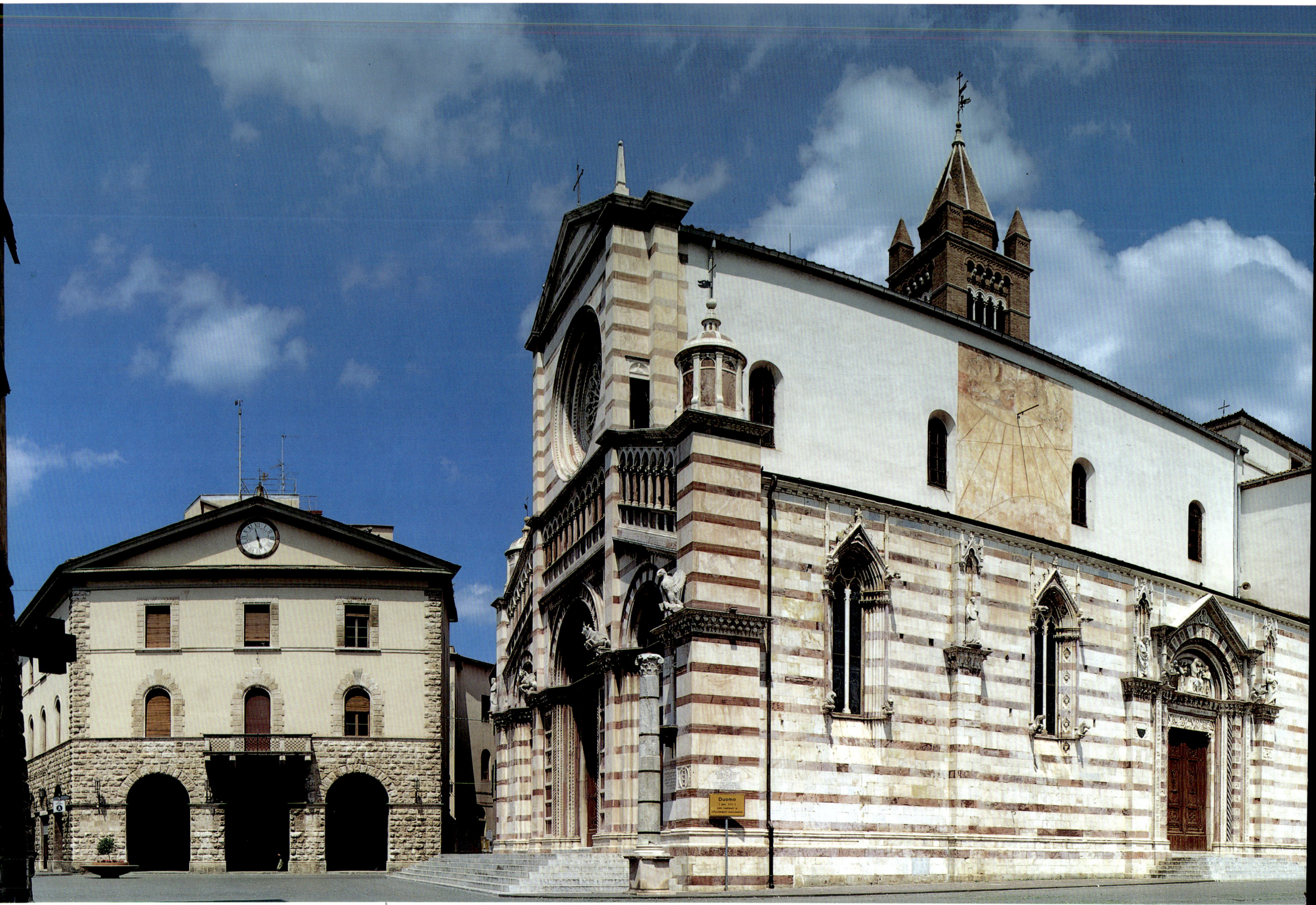

20.

22.

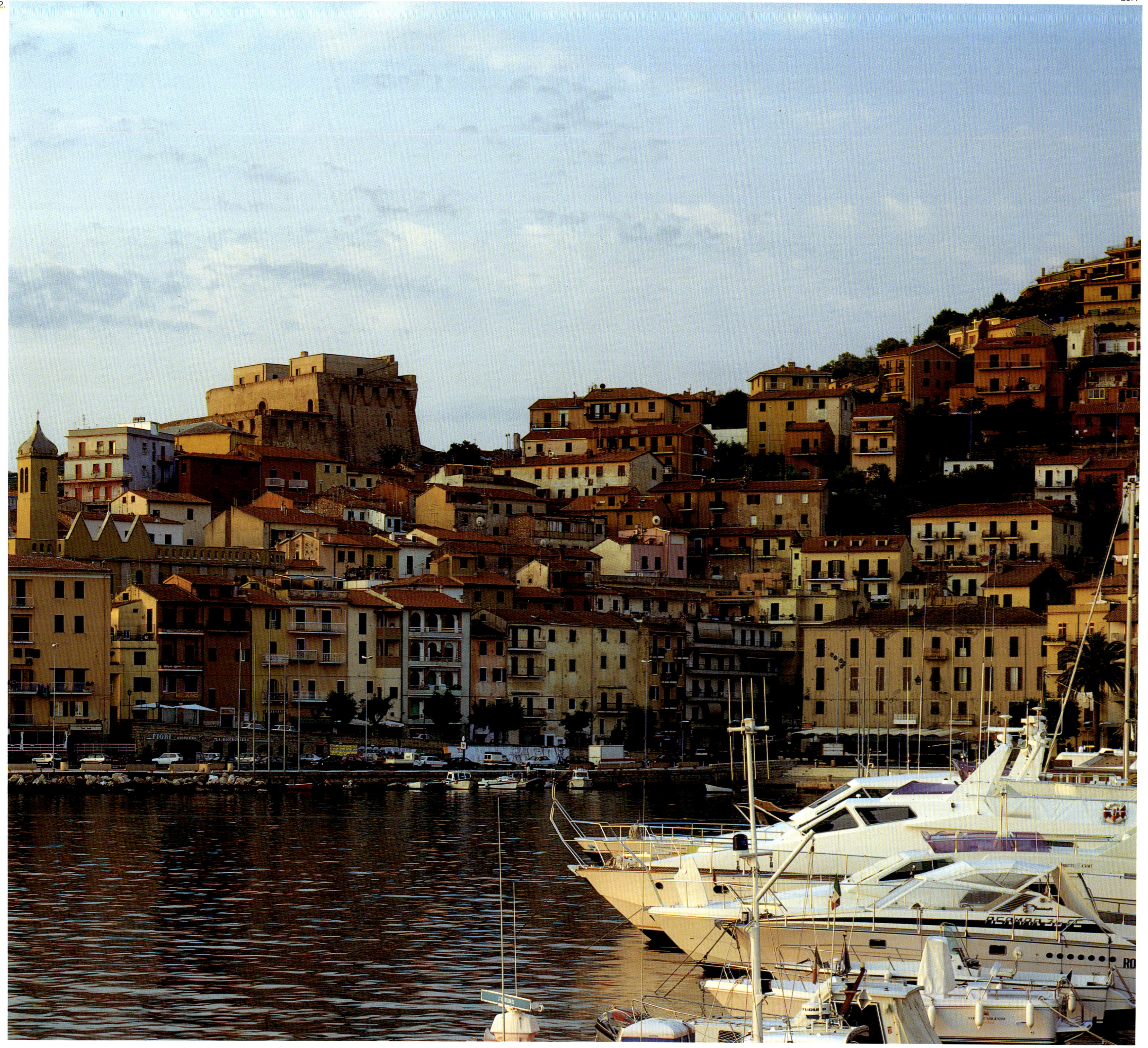

23. ▶

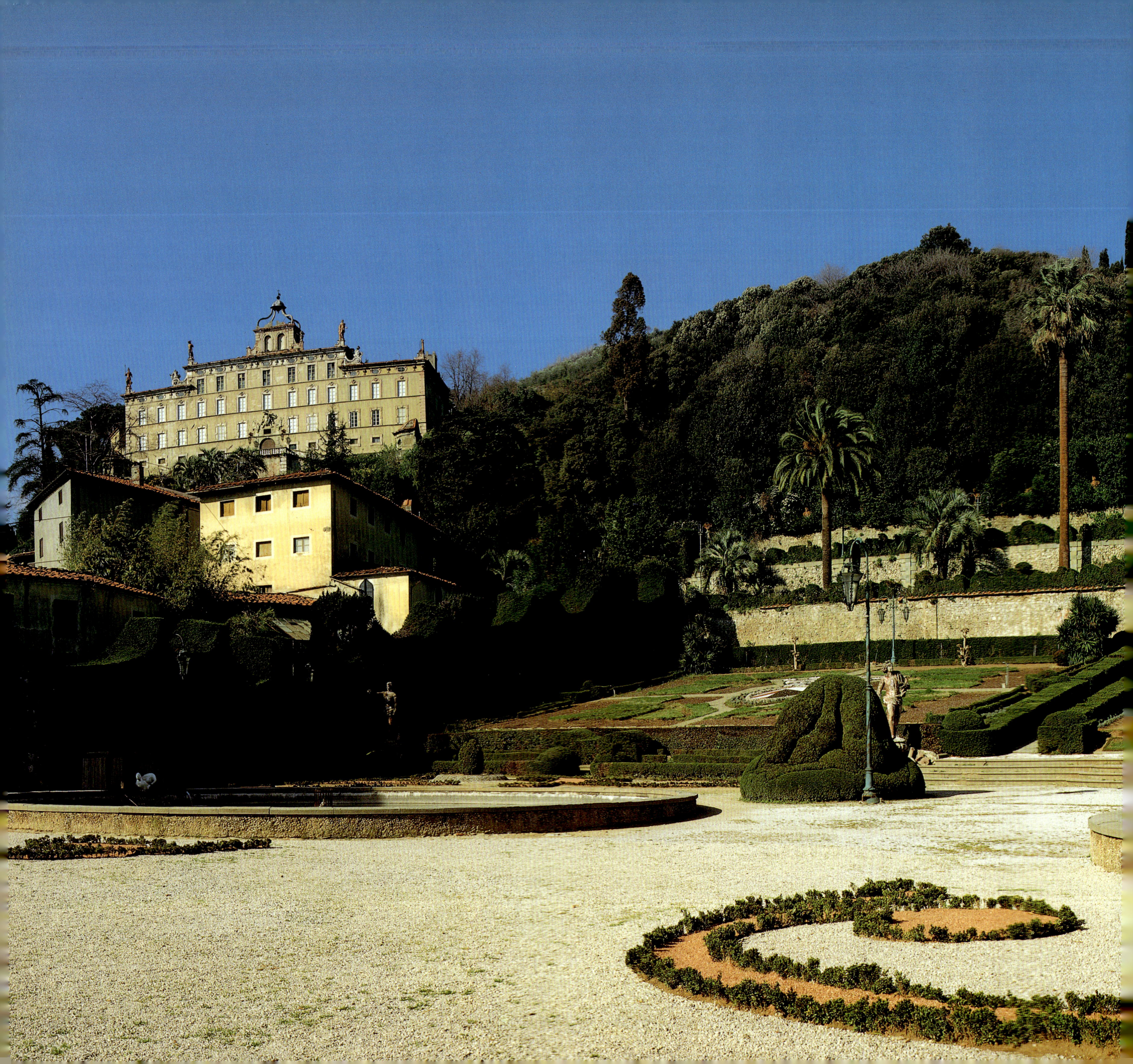

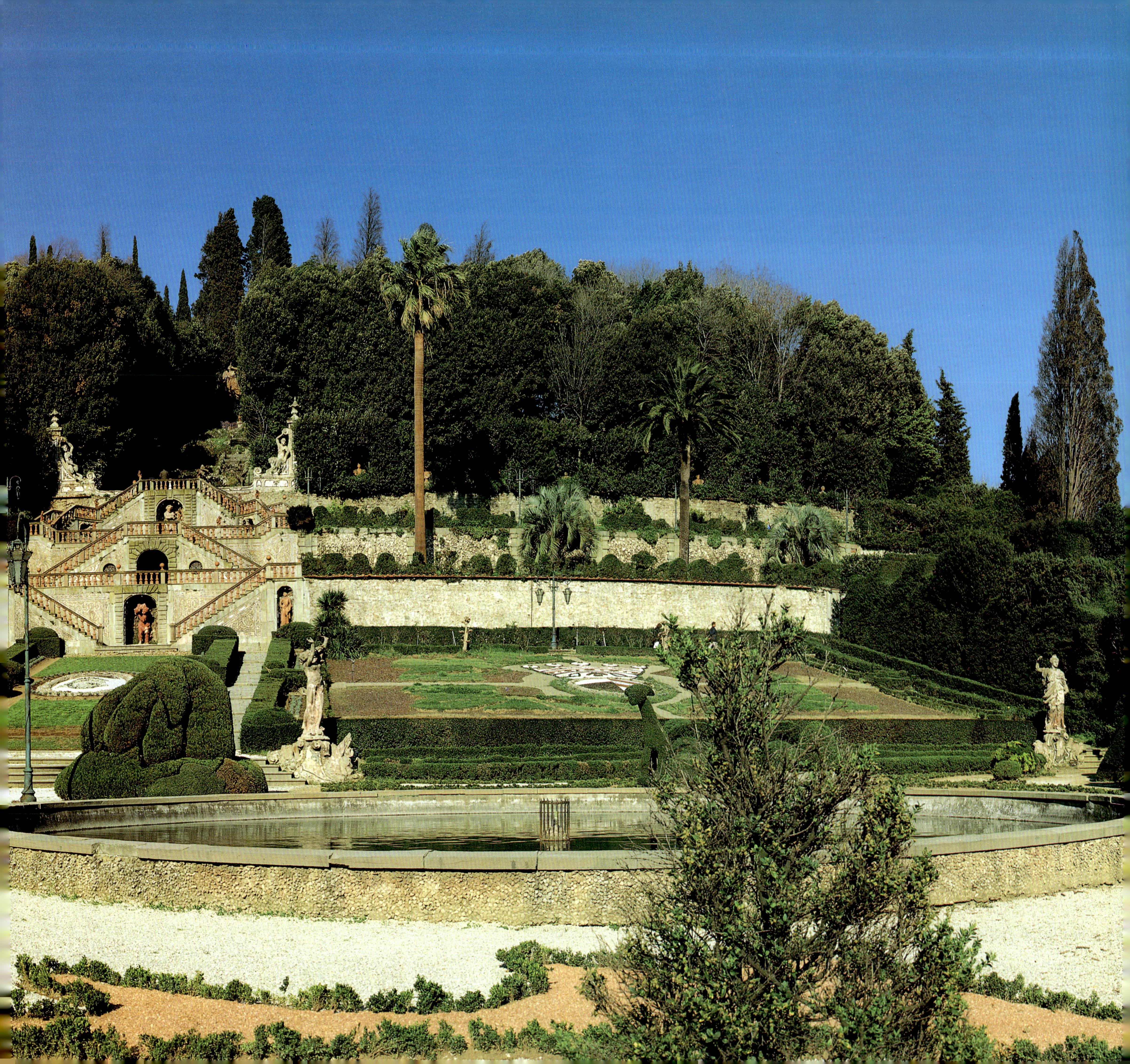

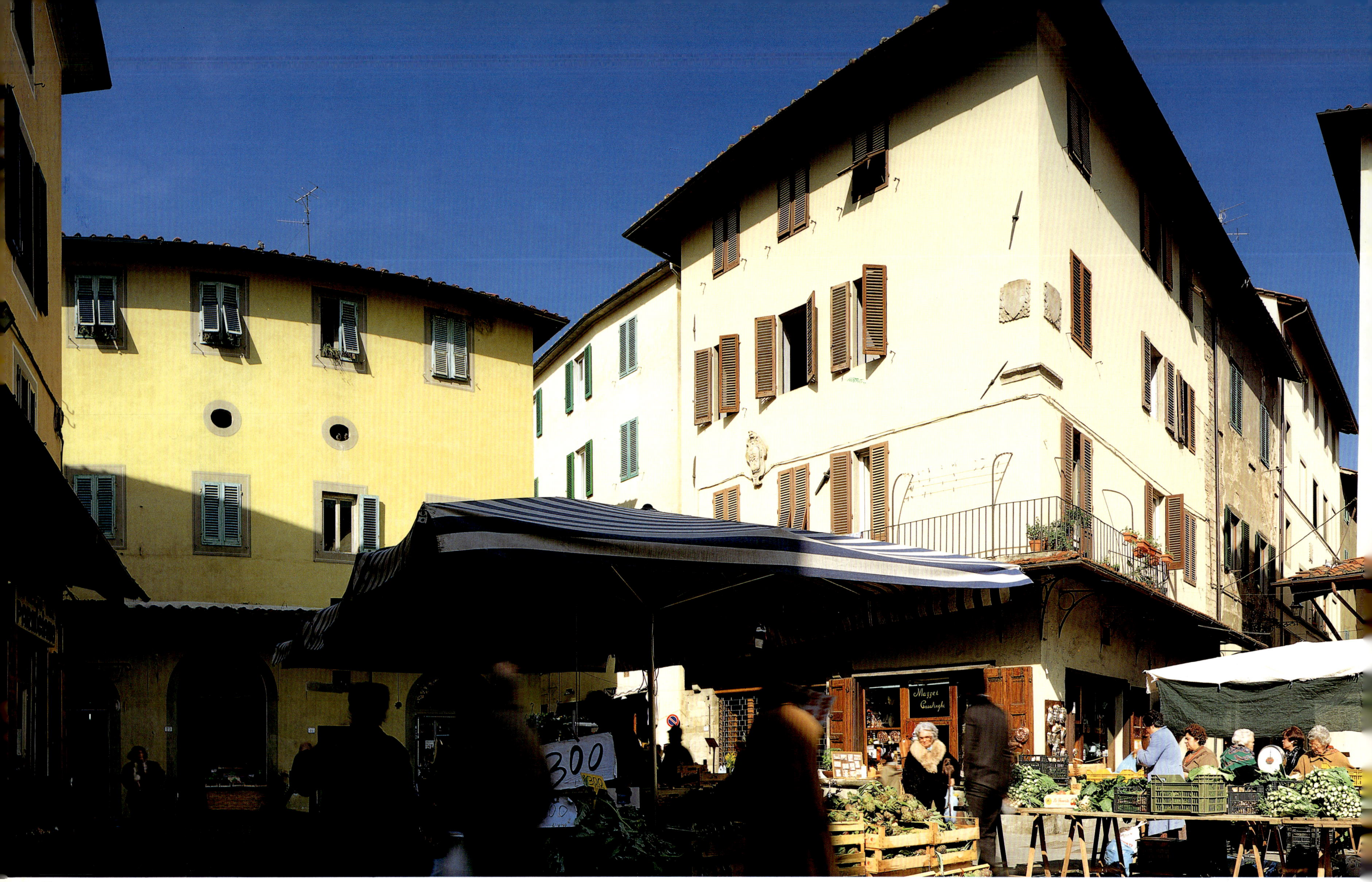

24.

PISTOIA
OSPEDALE DEL CEPPO

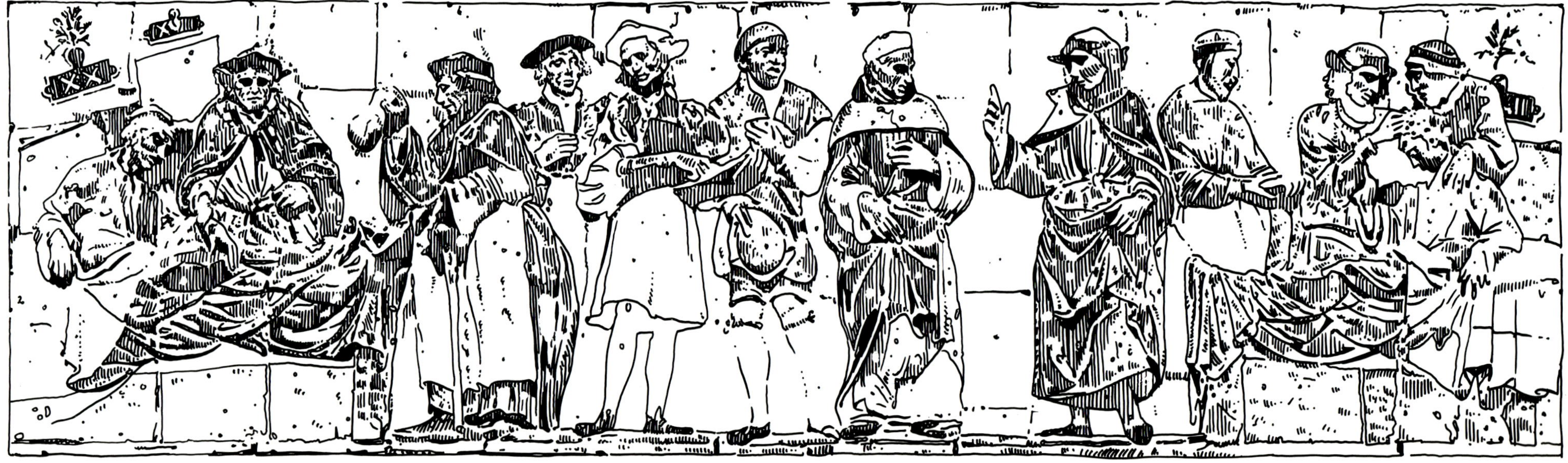

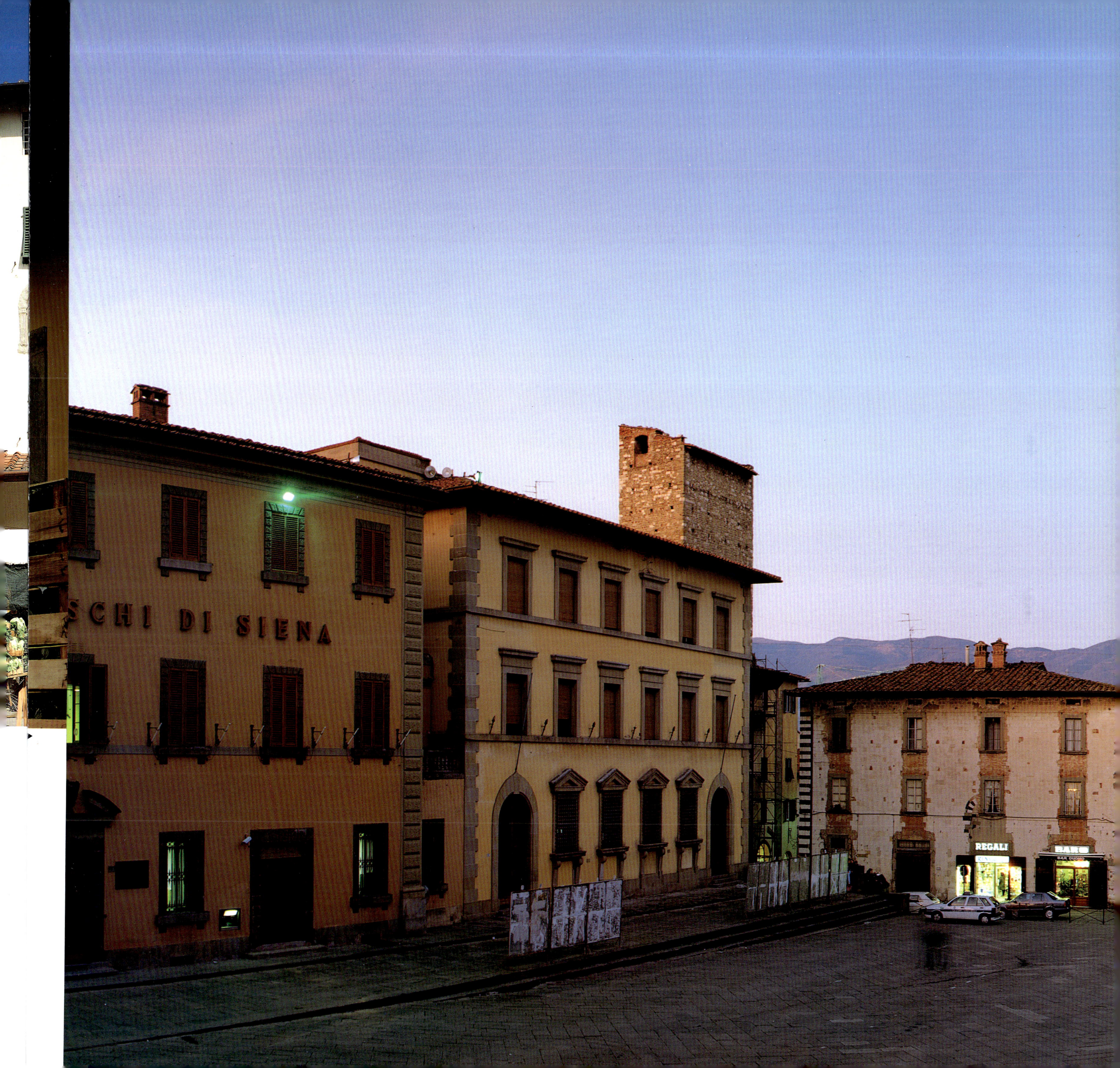
SCHI DI SIENA
REGALI

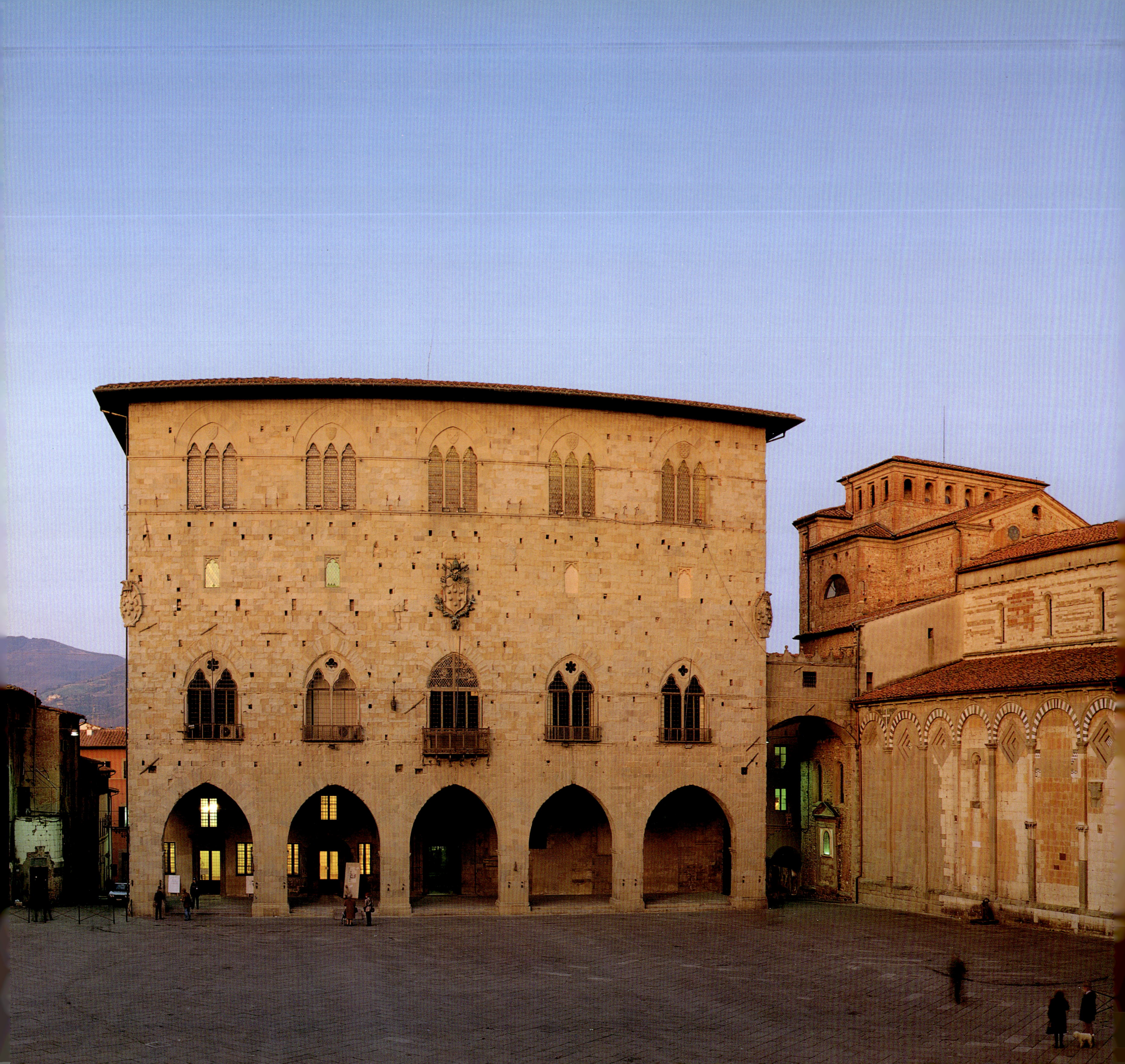

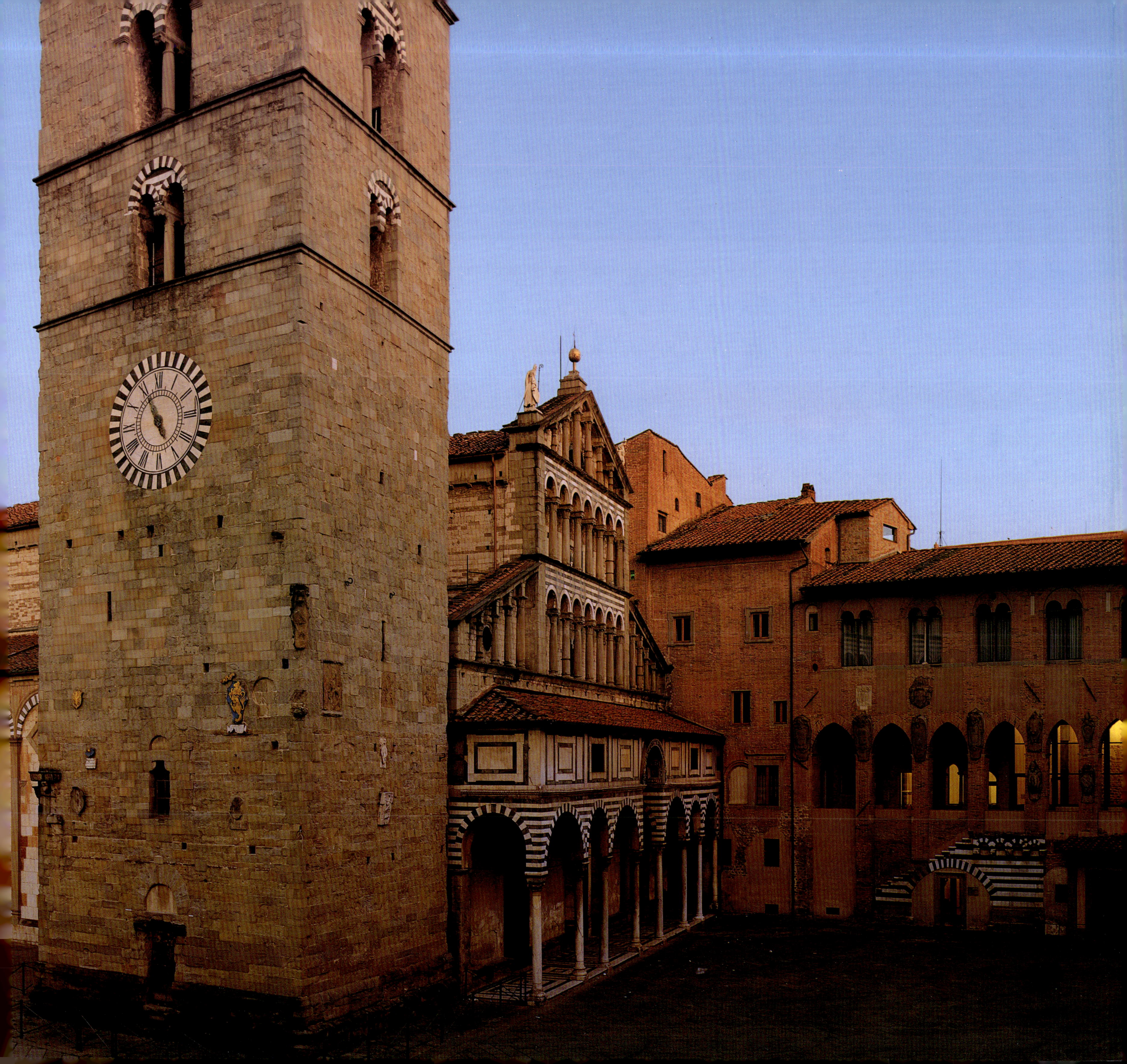

26.

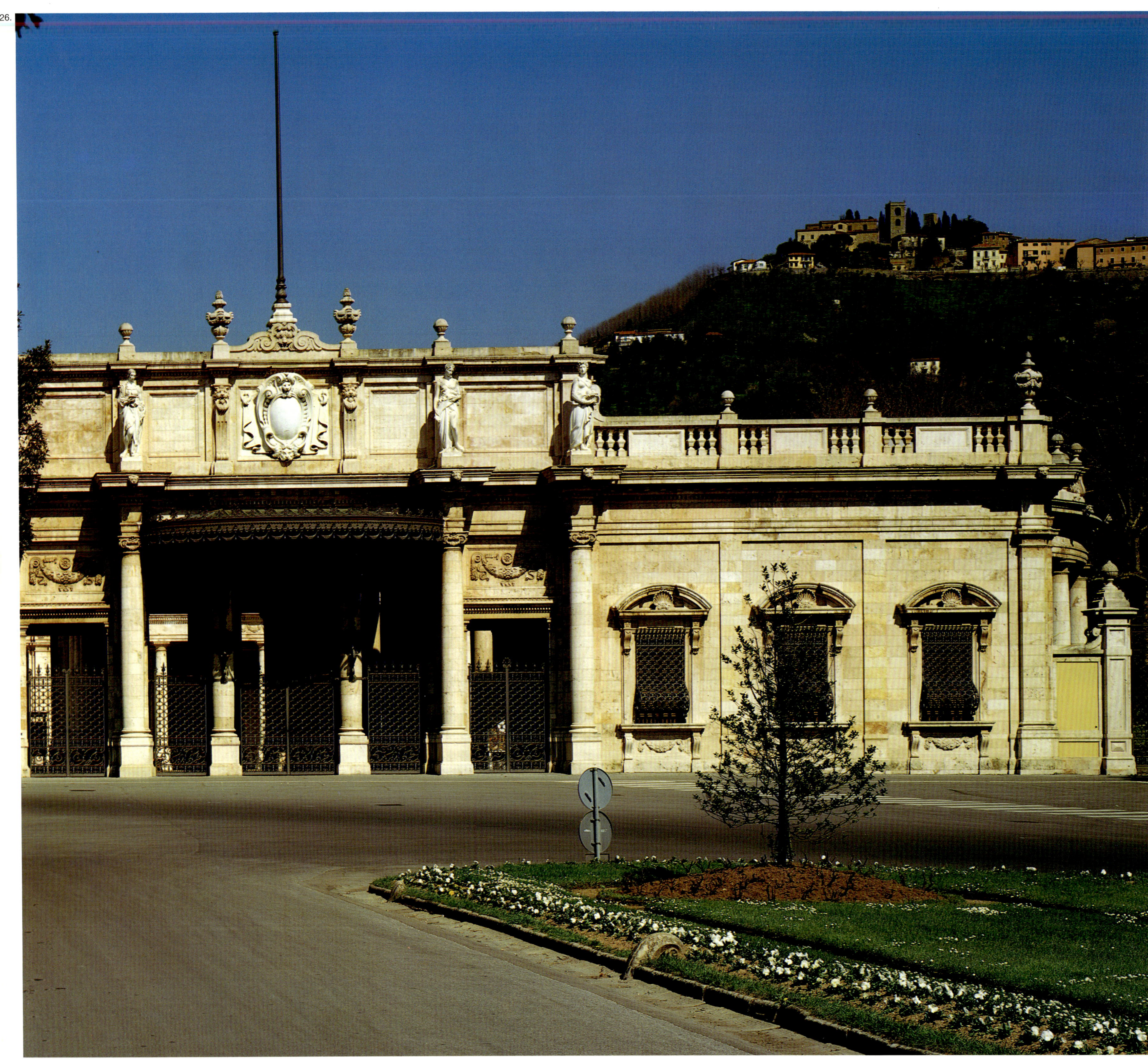

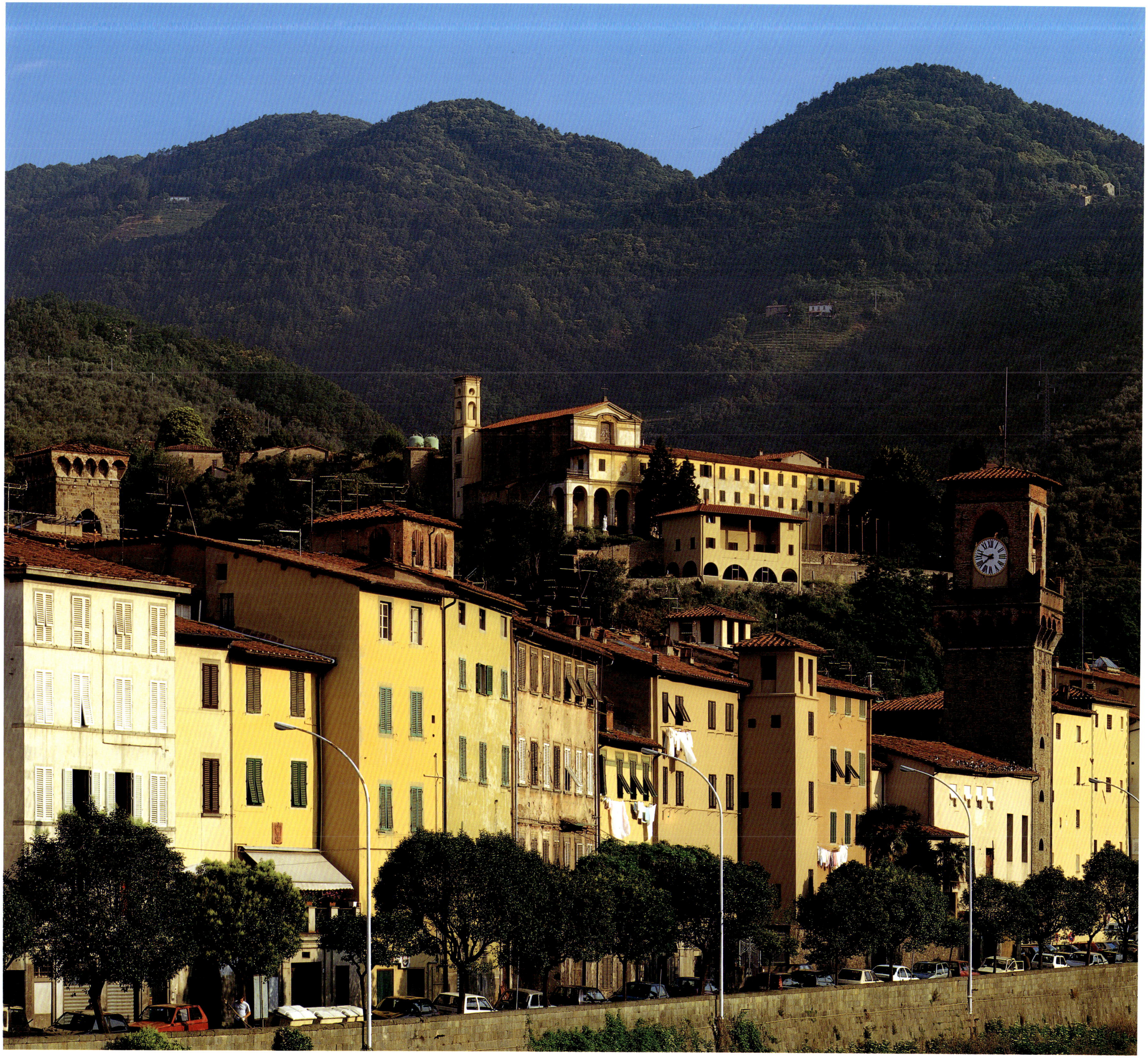

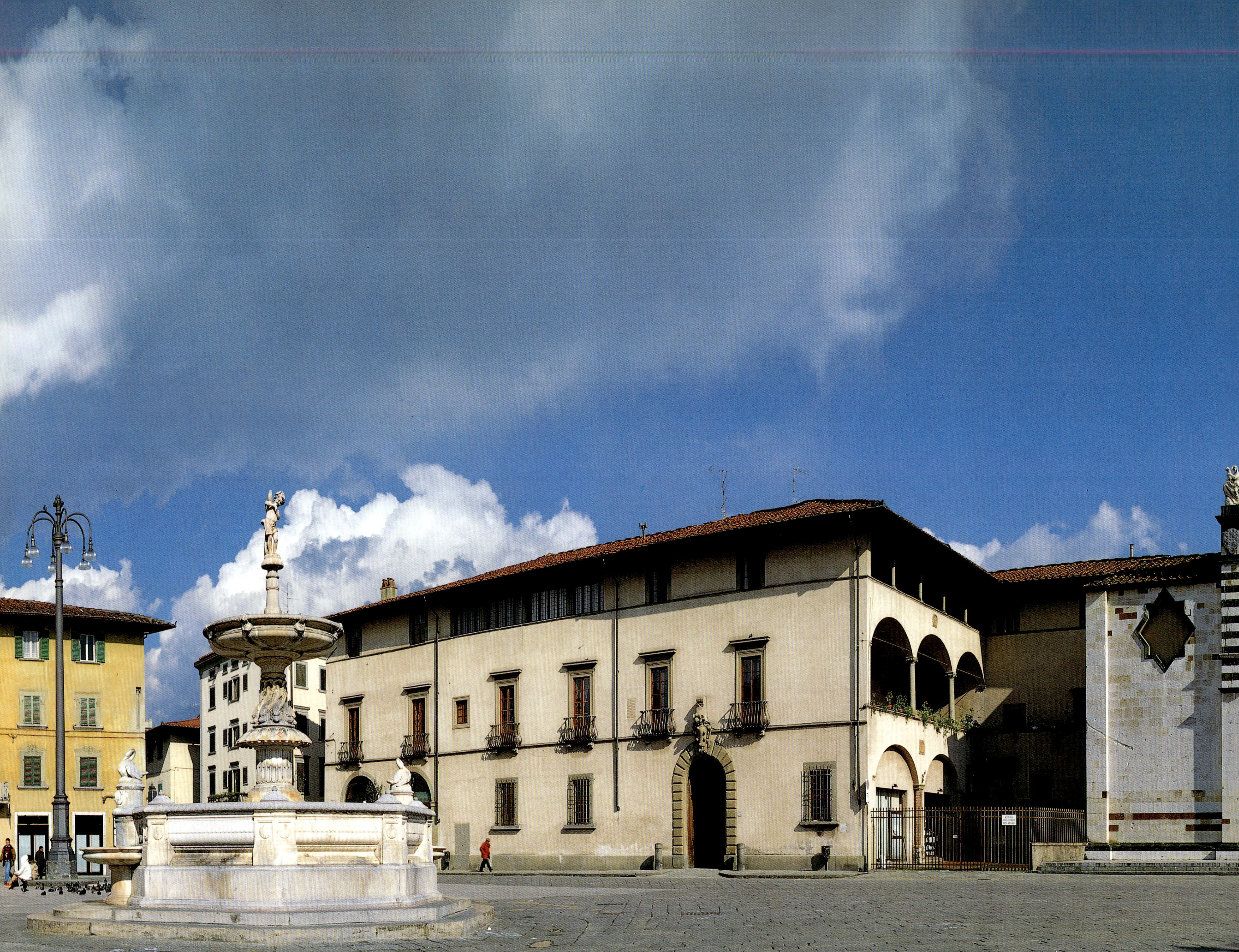

28.

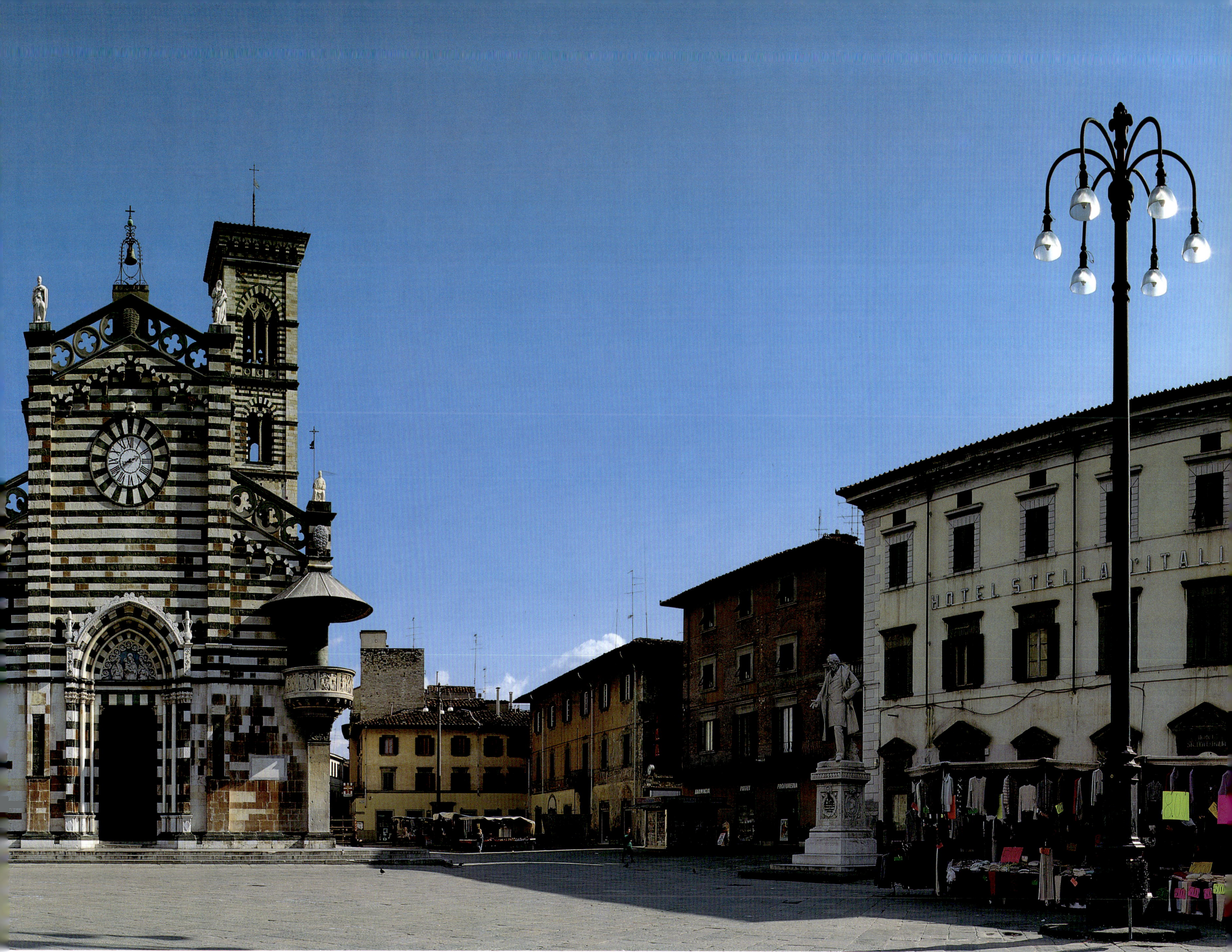
HOTEL STELLA
'ITALI

29.

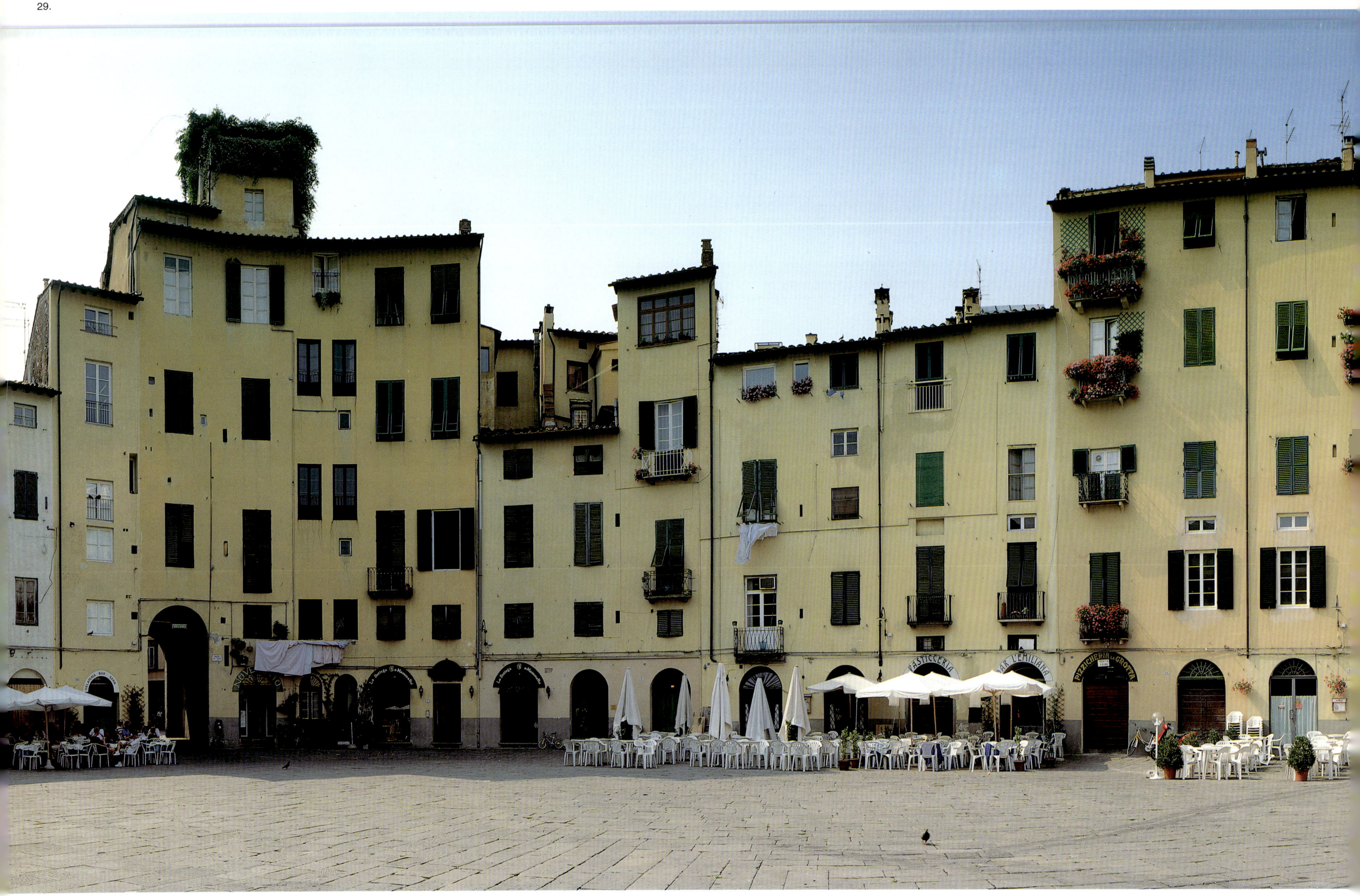

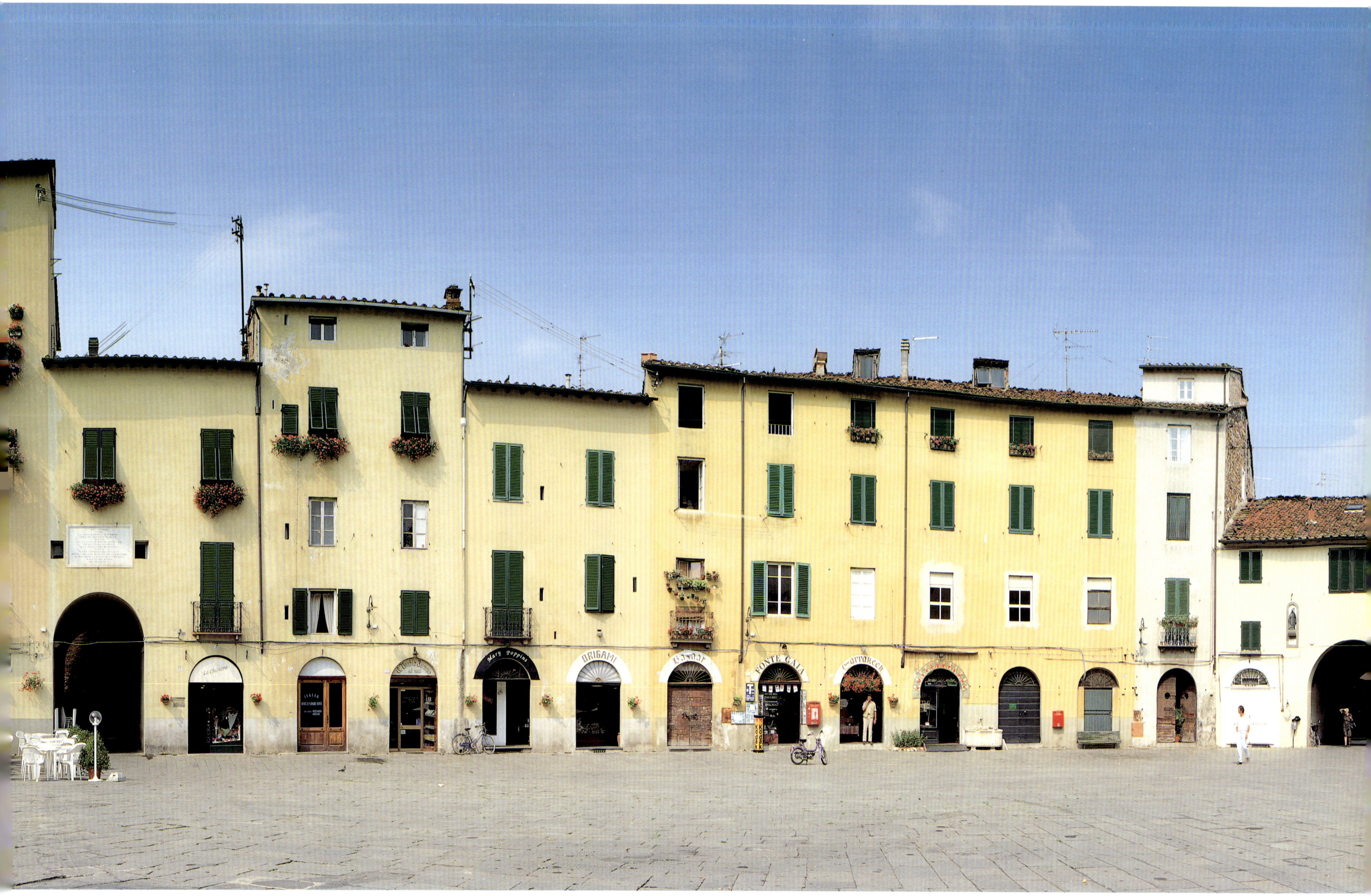

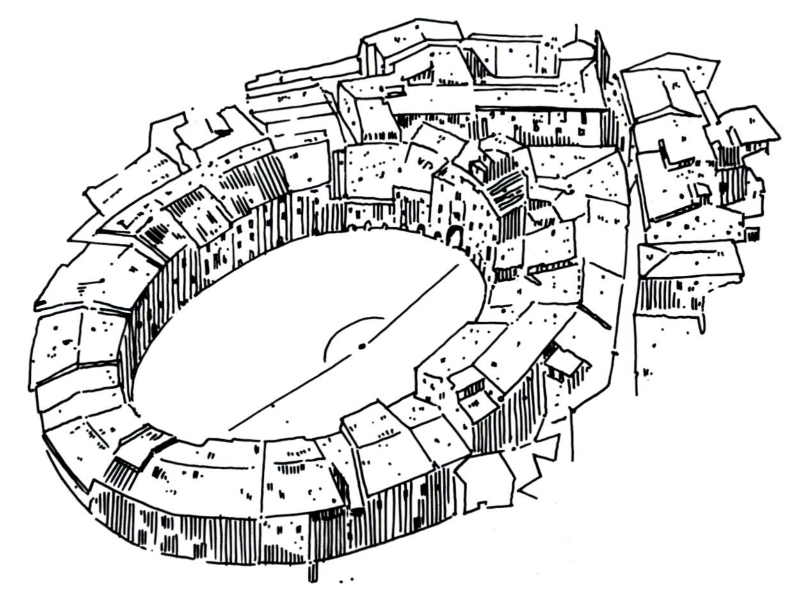

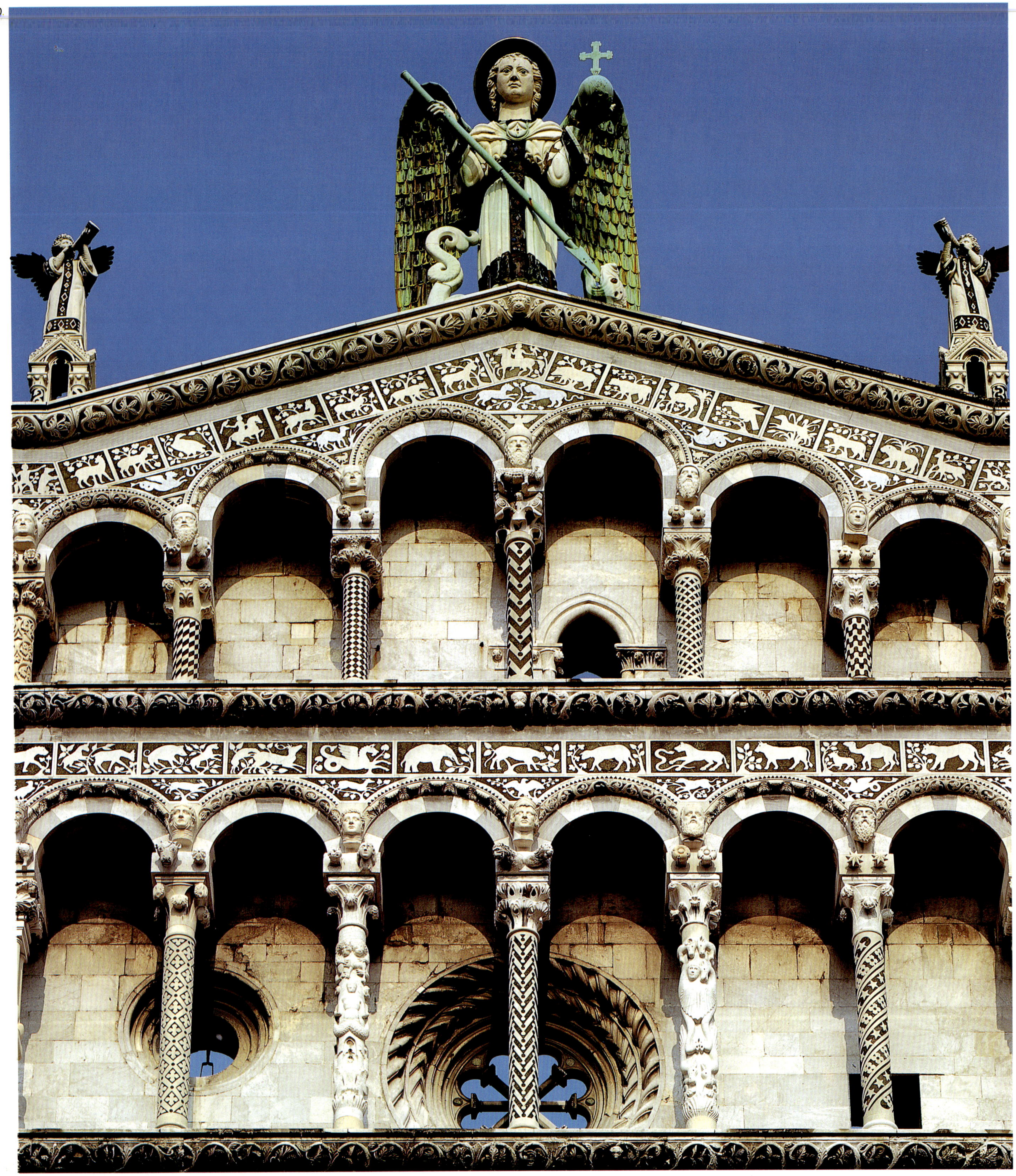

31.

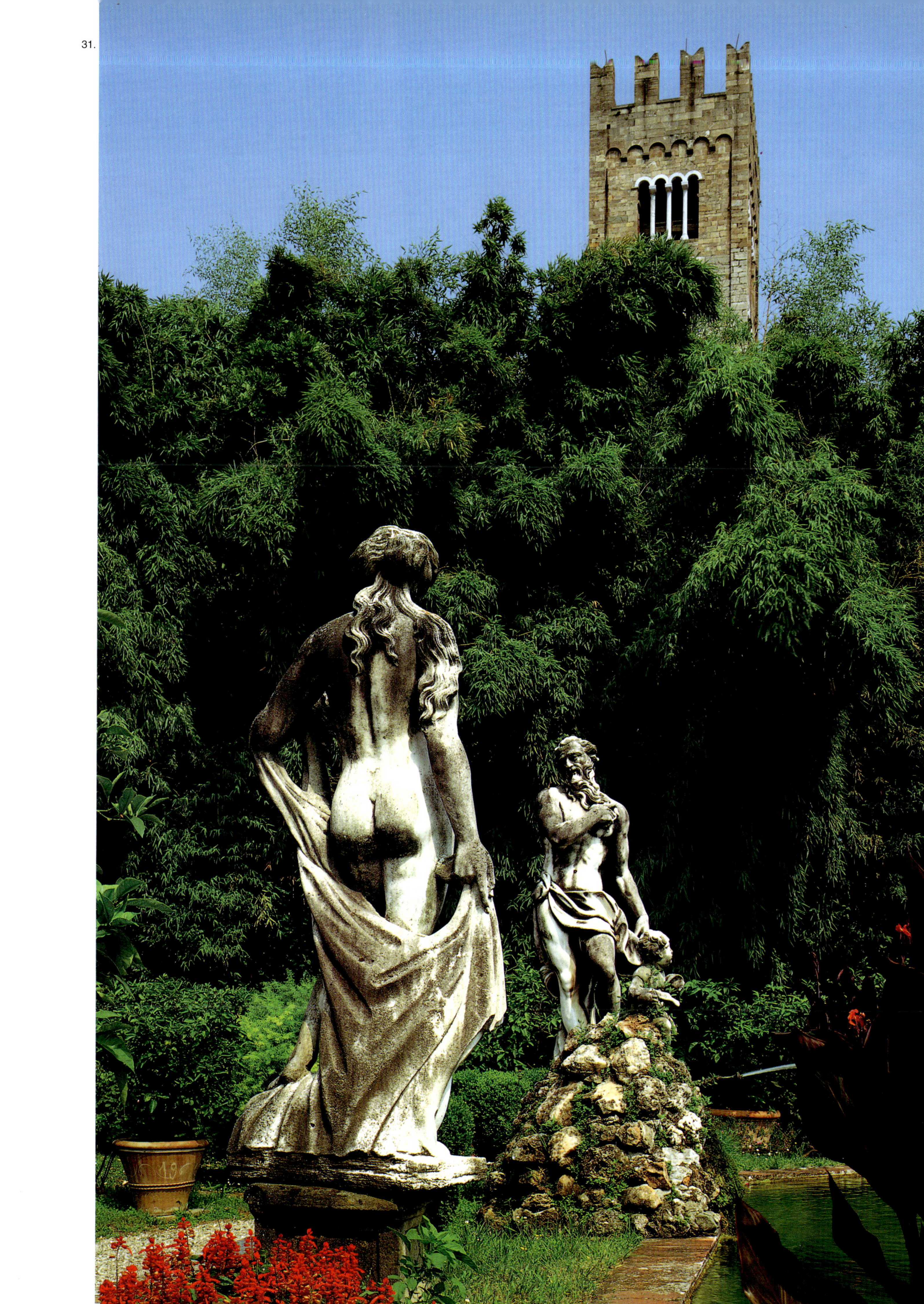

32.

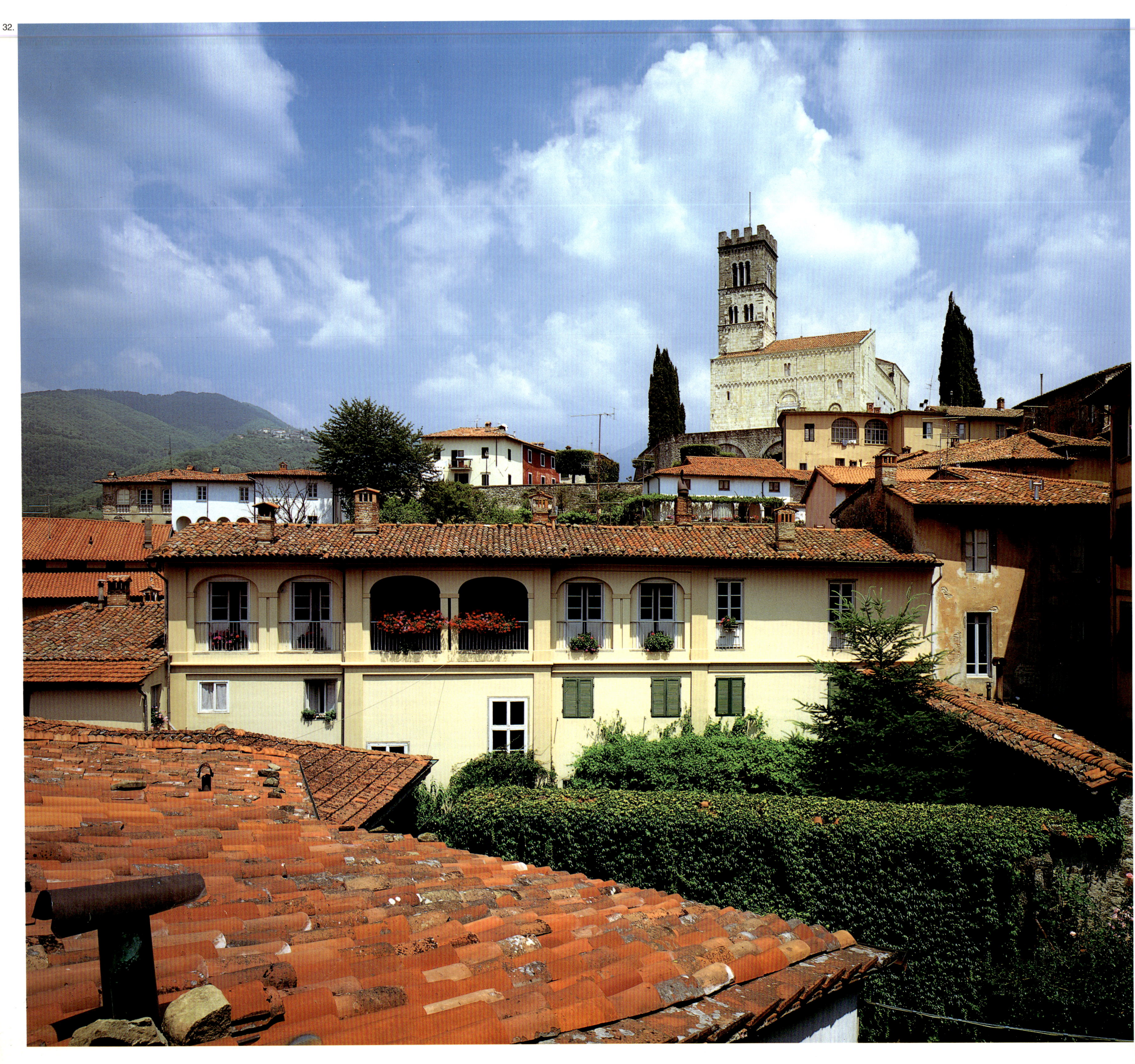

33.

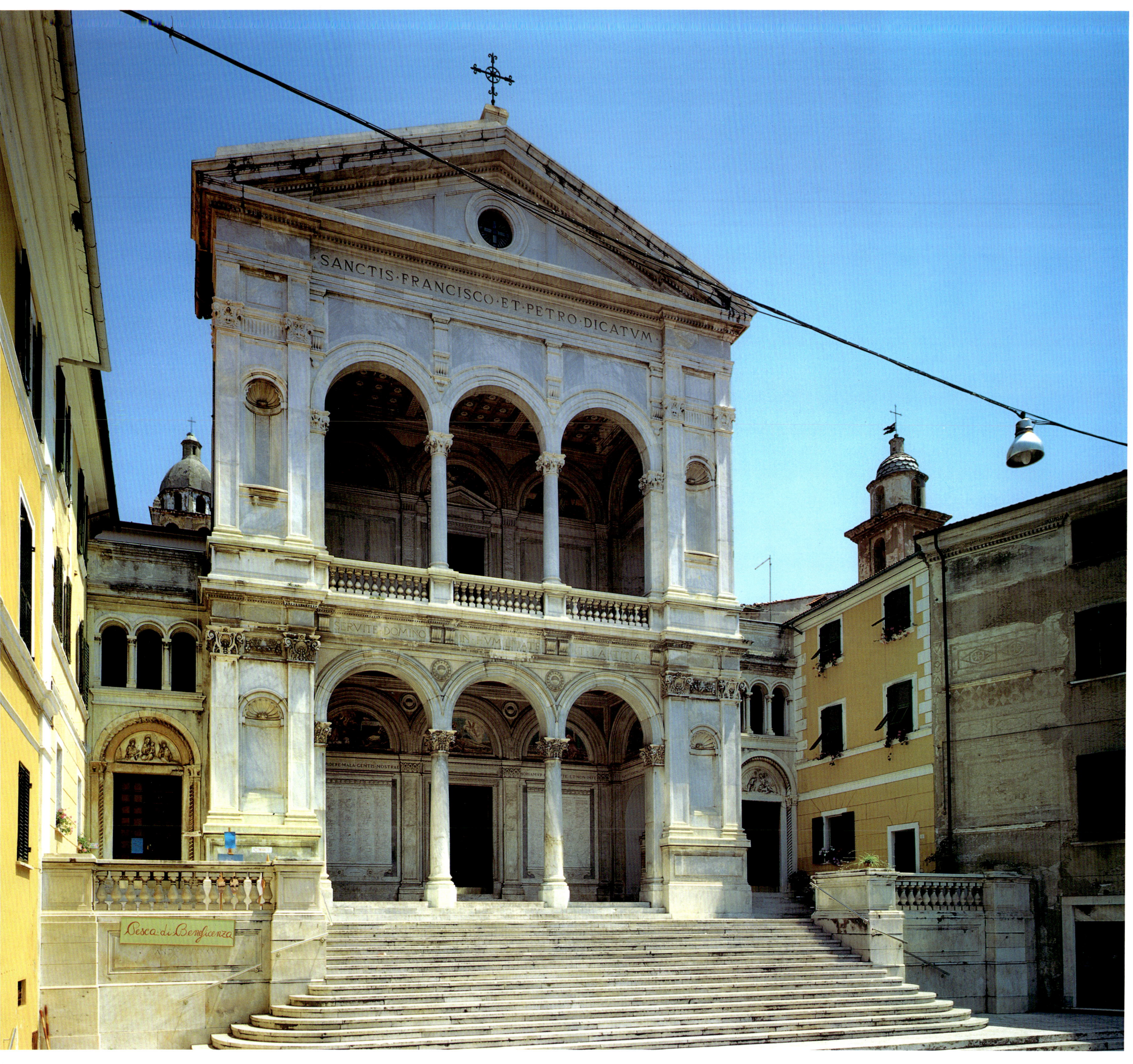
SANCTIS·FRANCISCO·ET·PETRO·DICATVM
SERVITE DOMINO
Pesca di Beneficenza

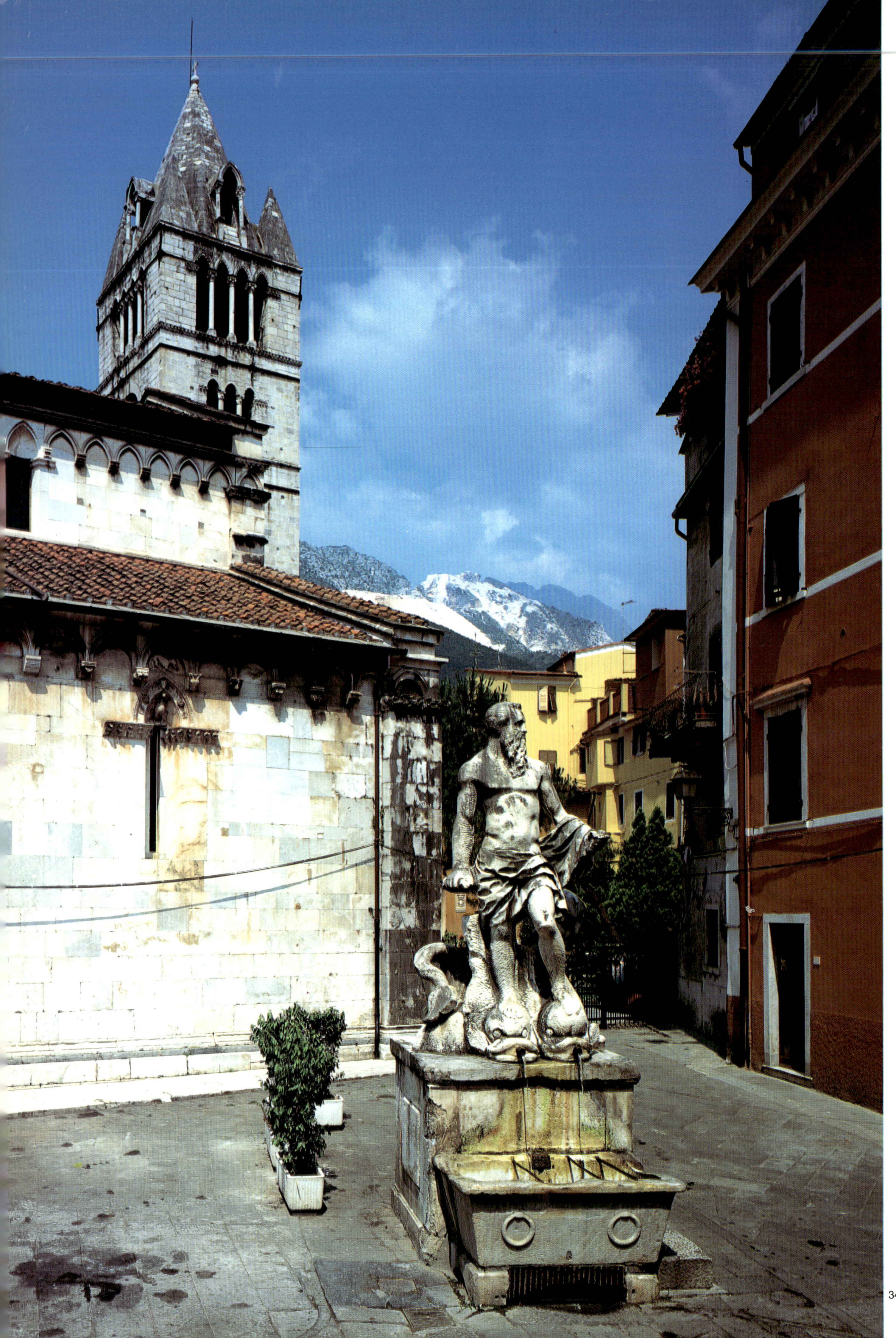

34.

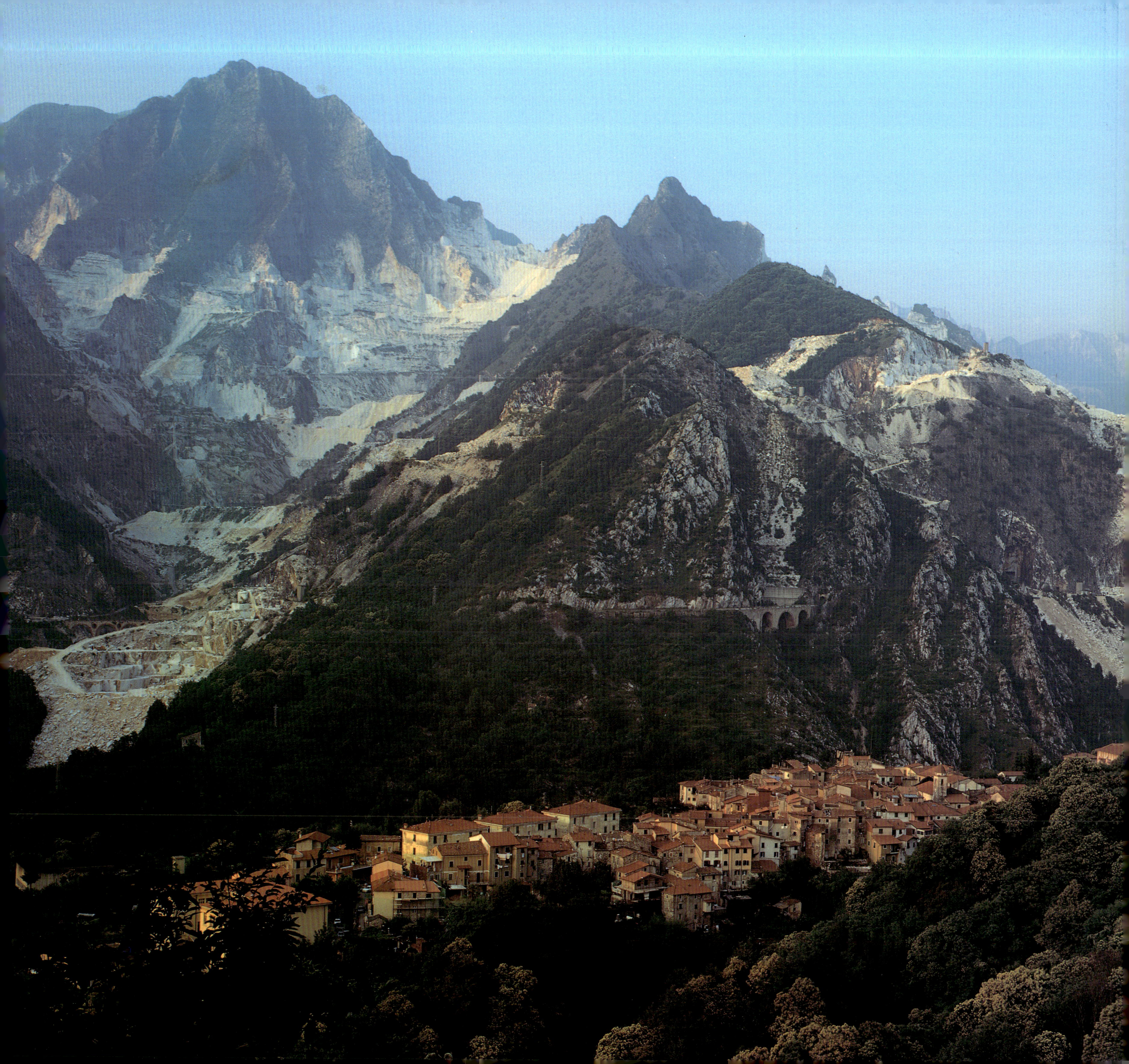

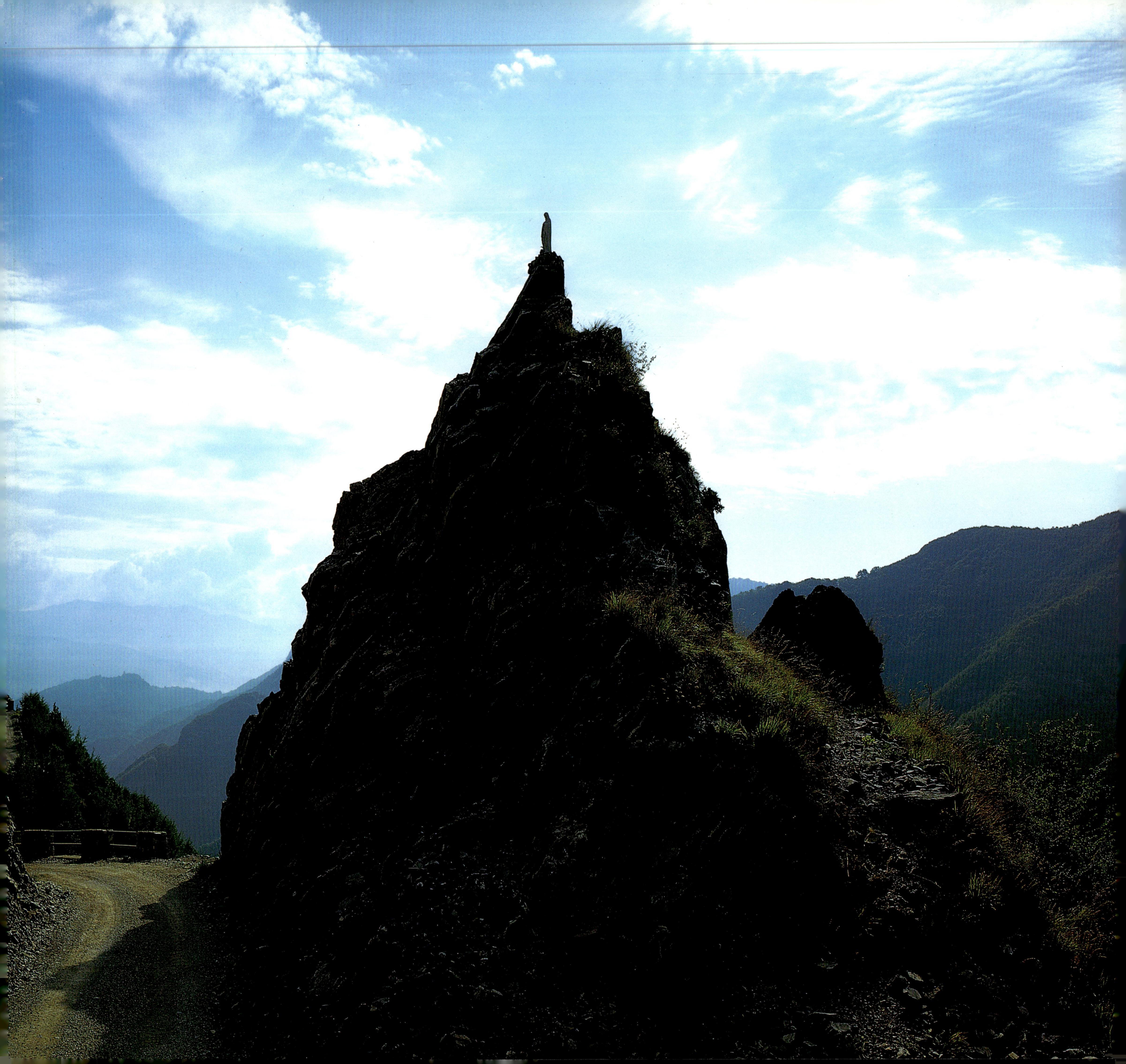

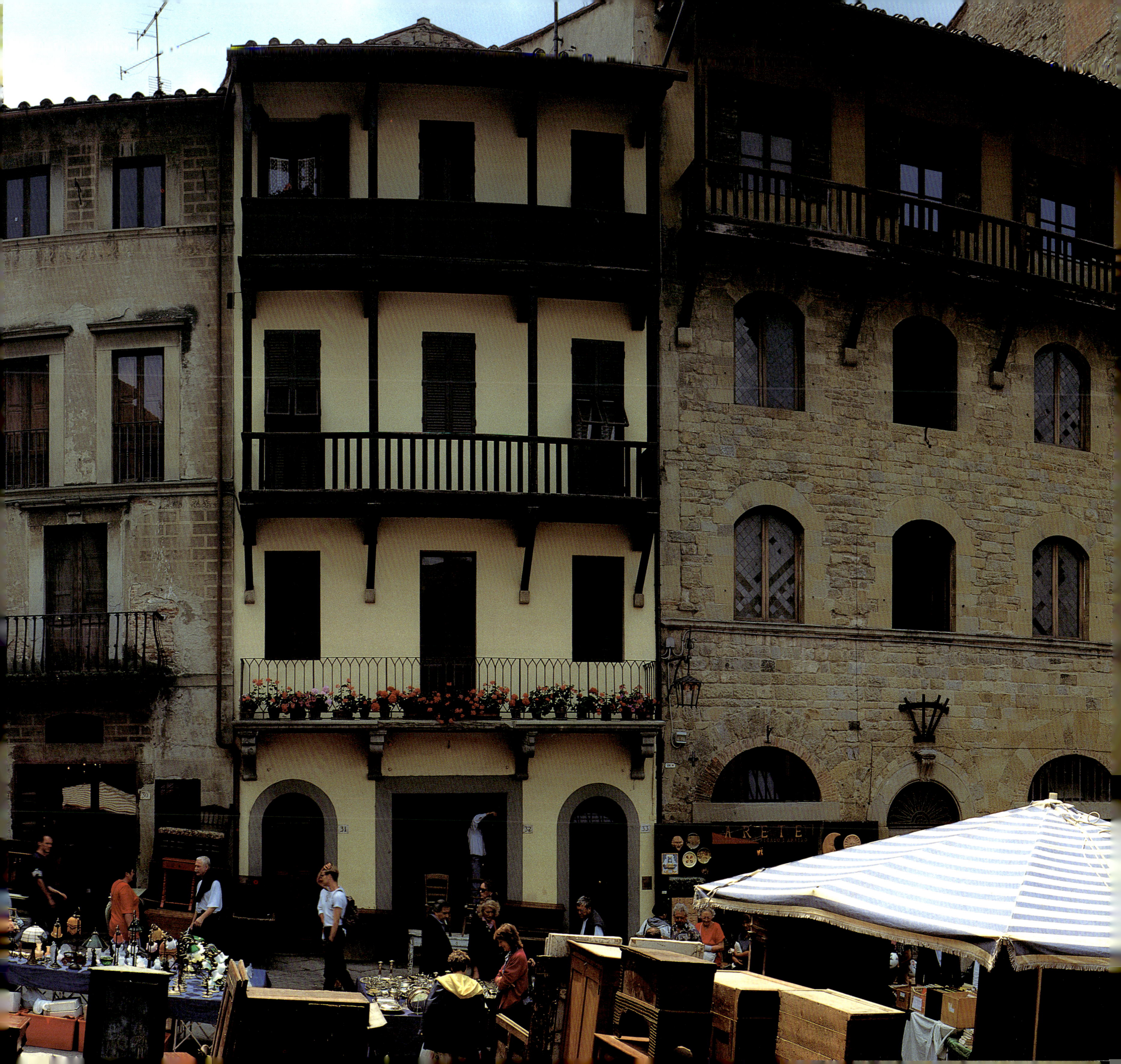
ARETE

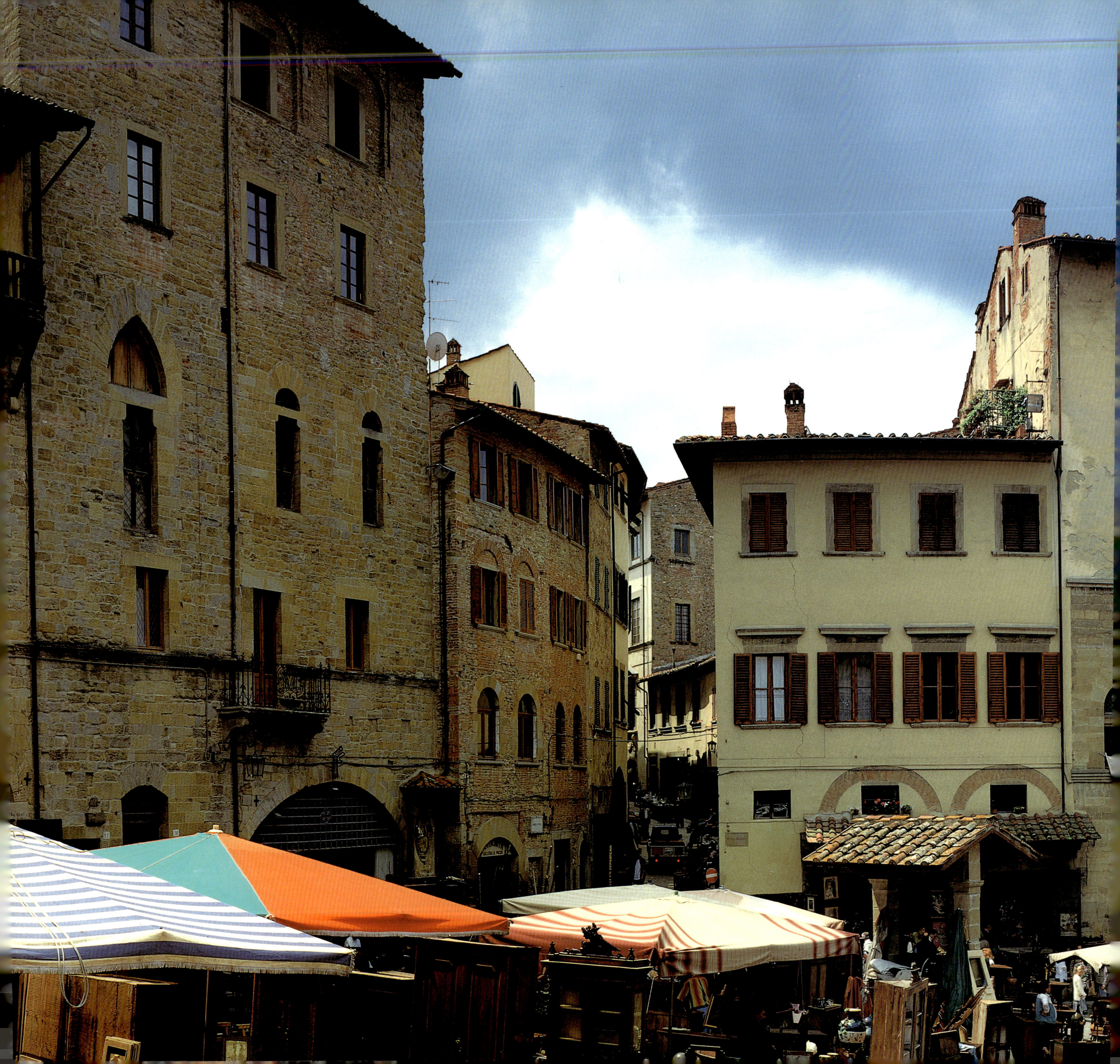

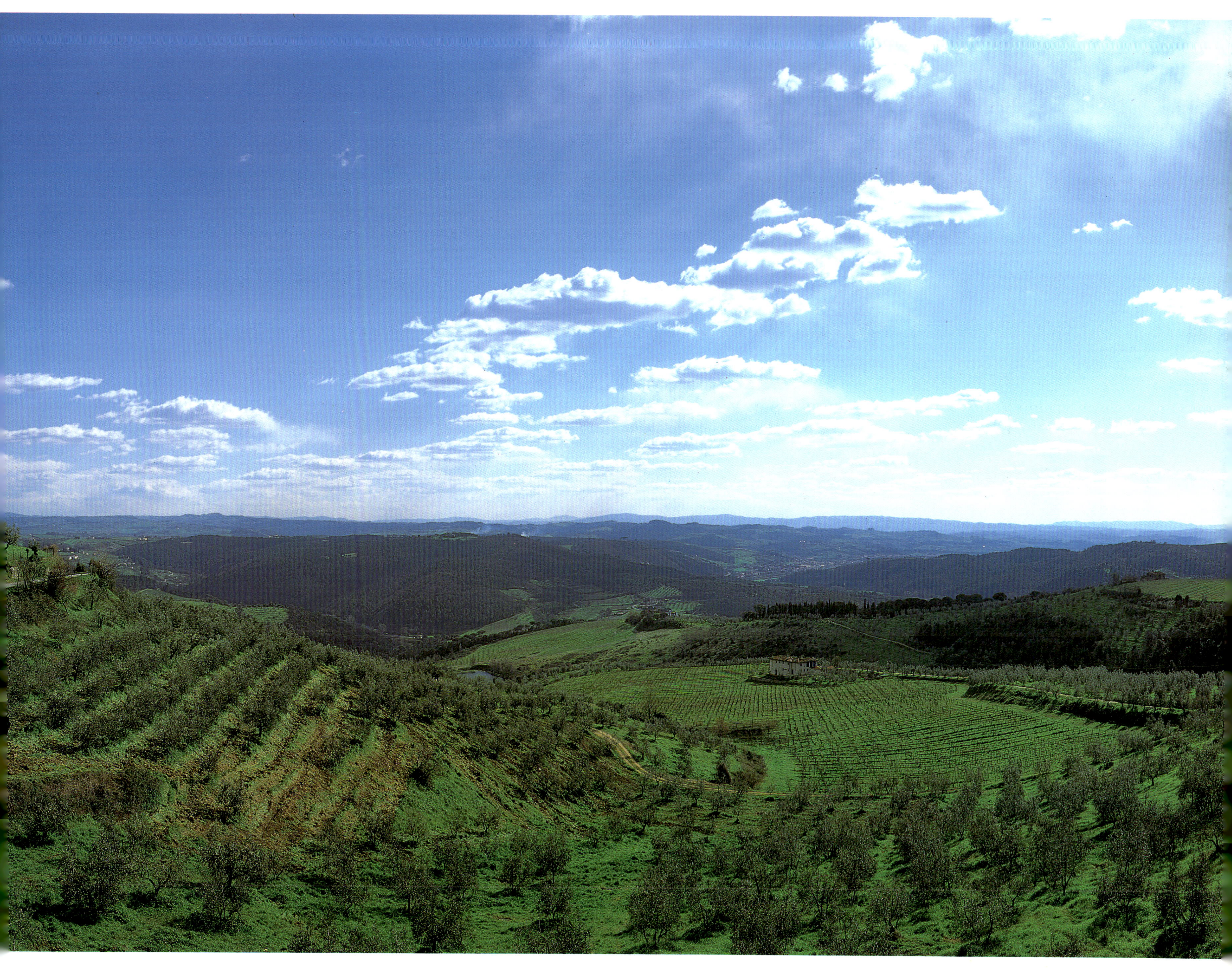

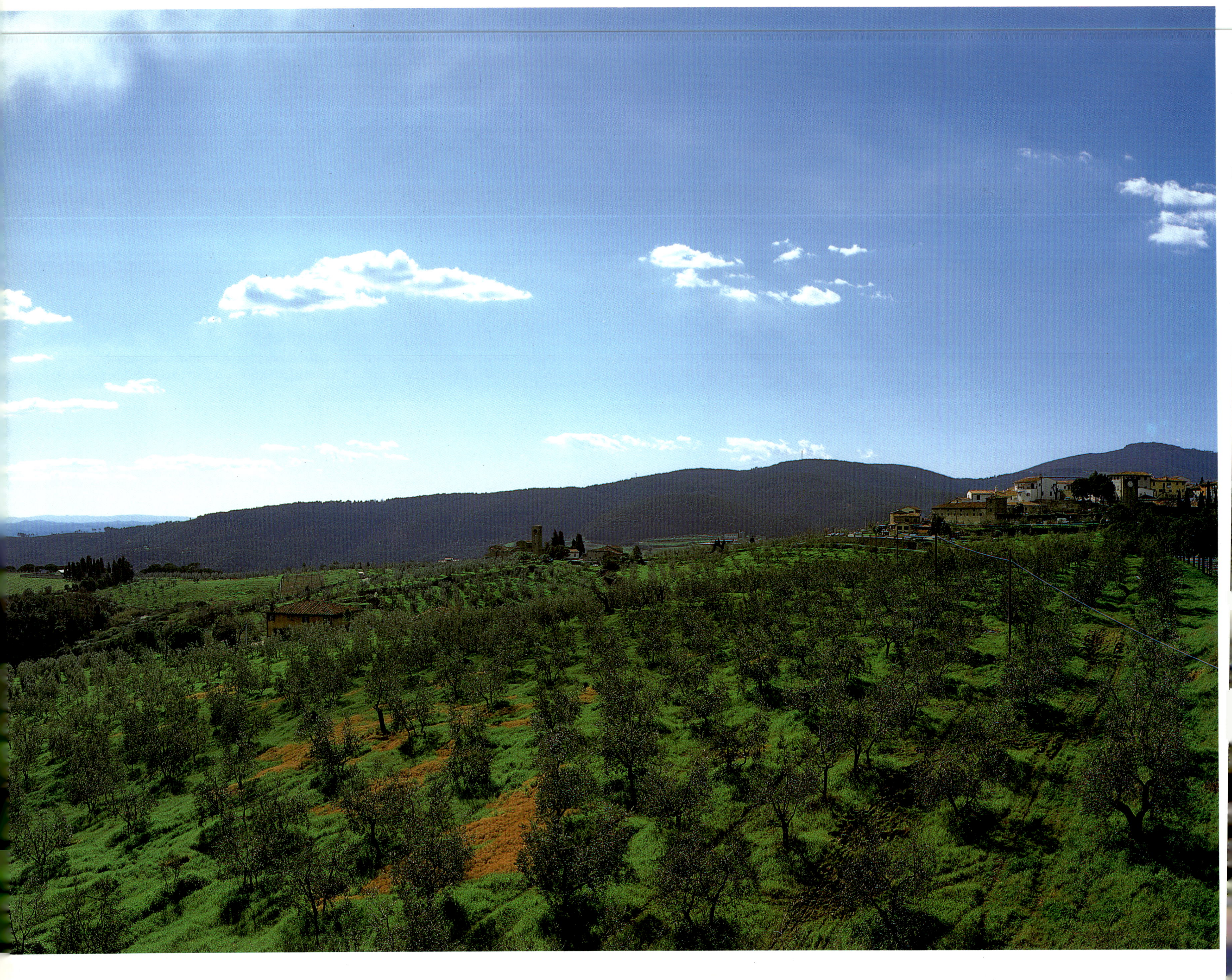

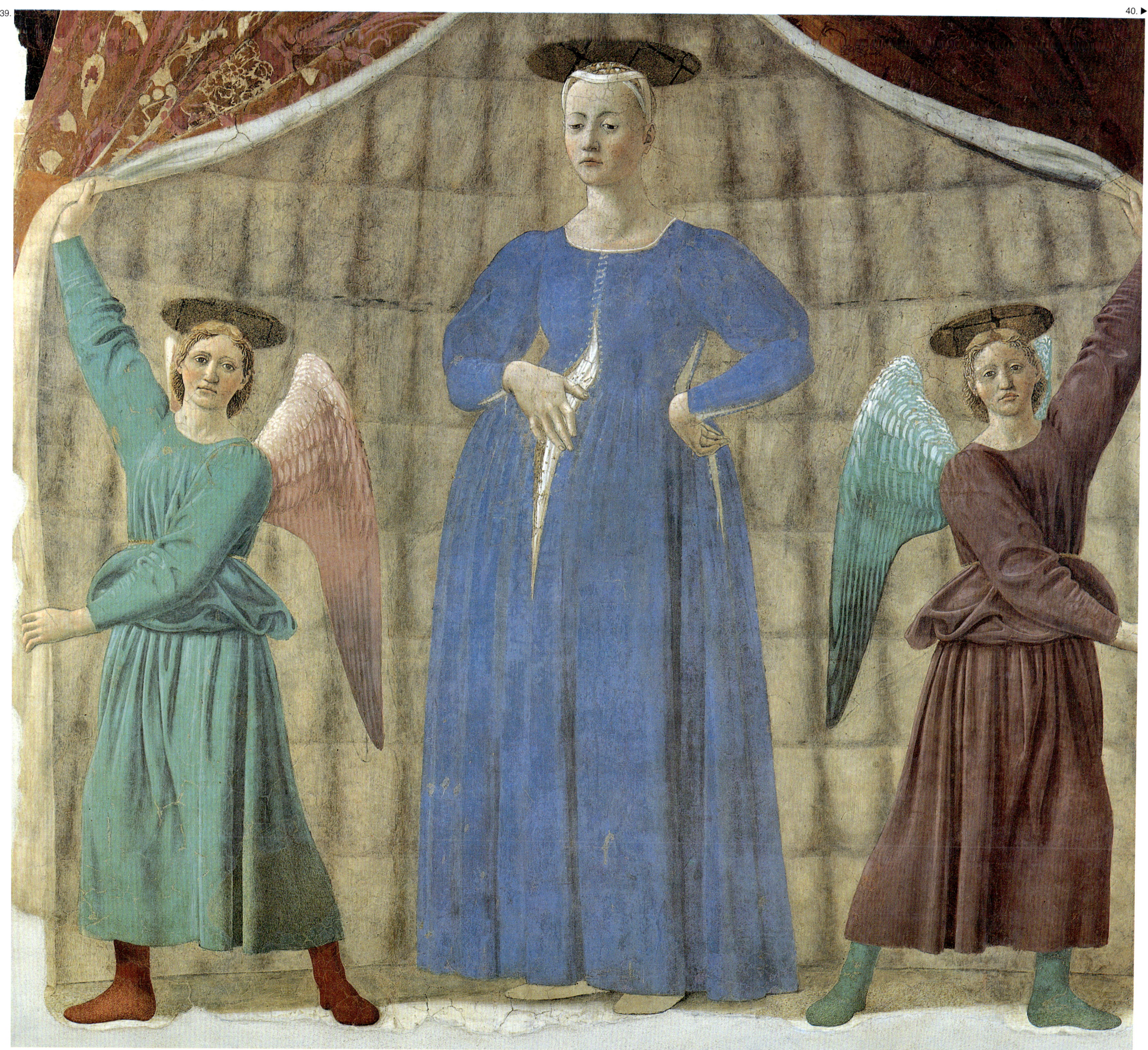

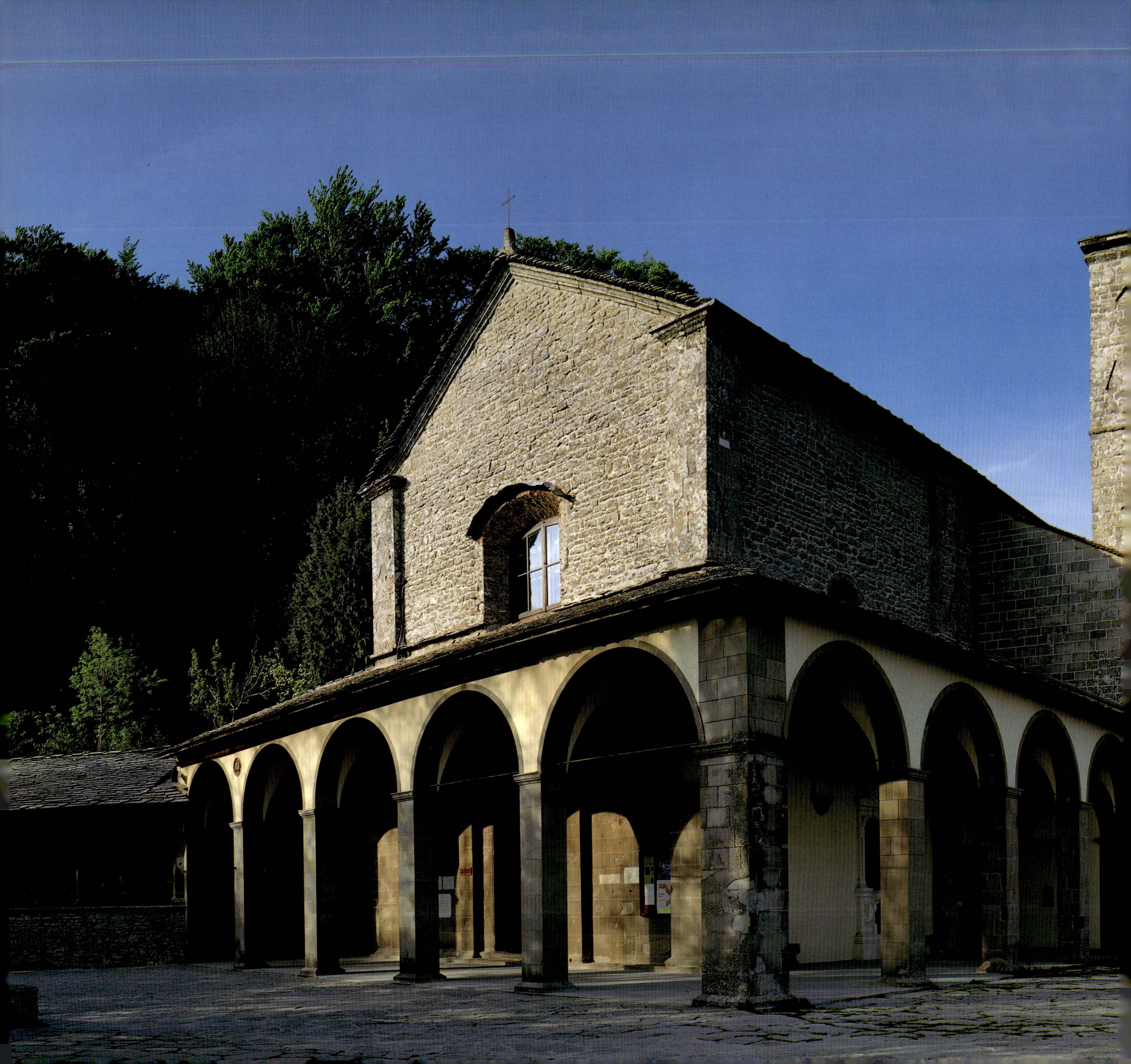

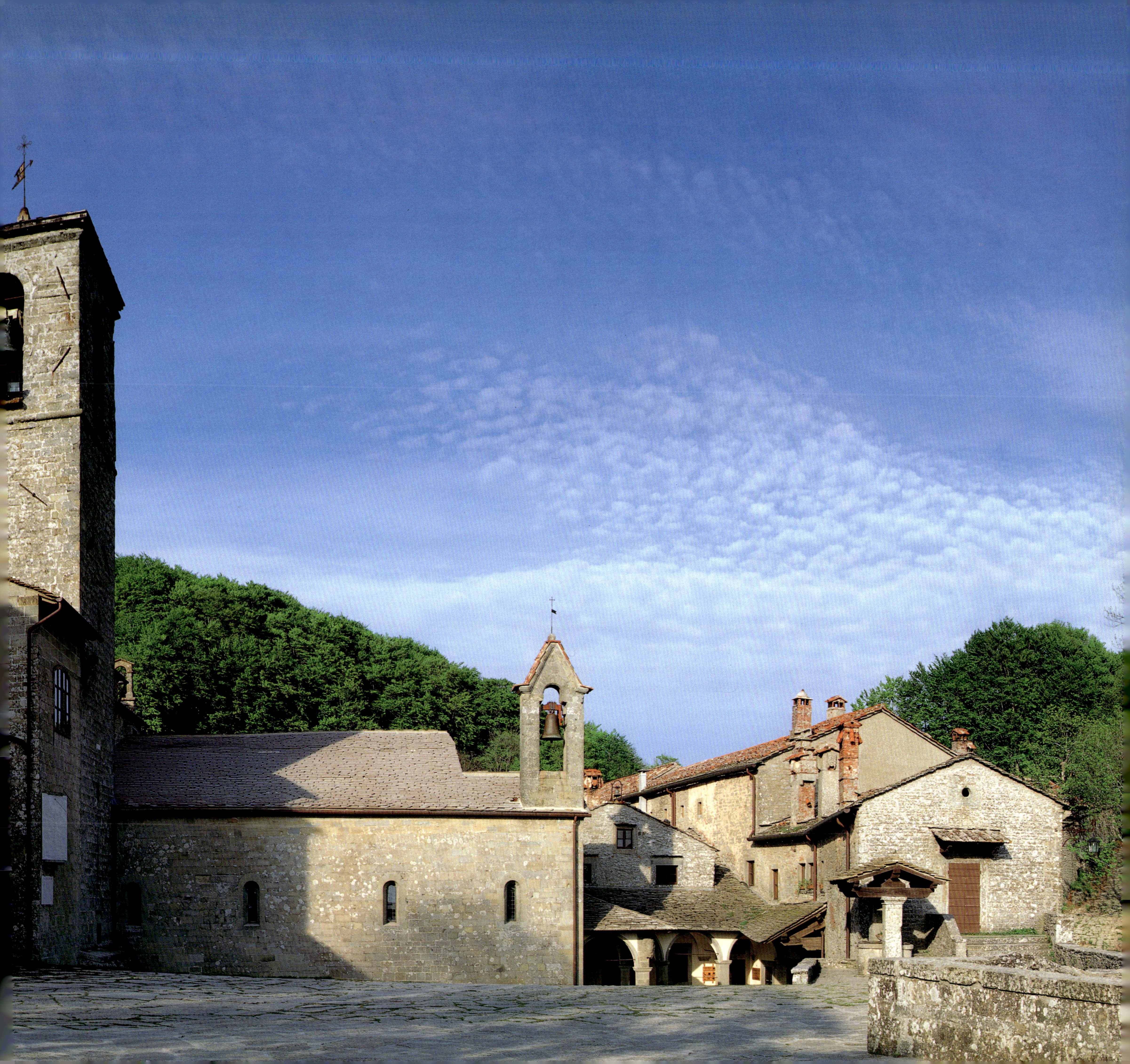

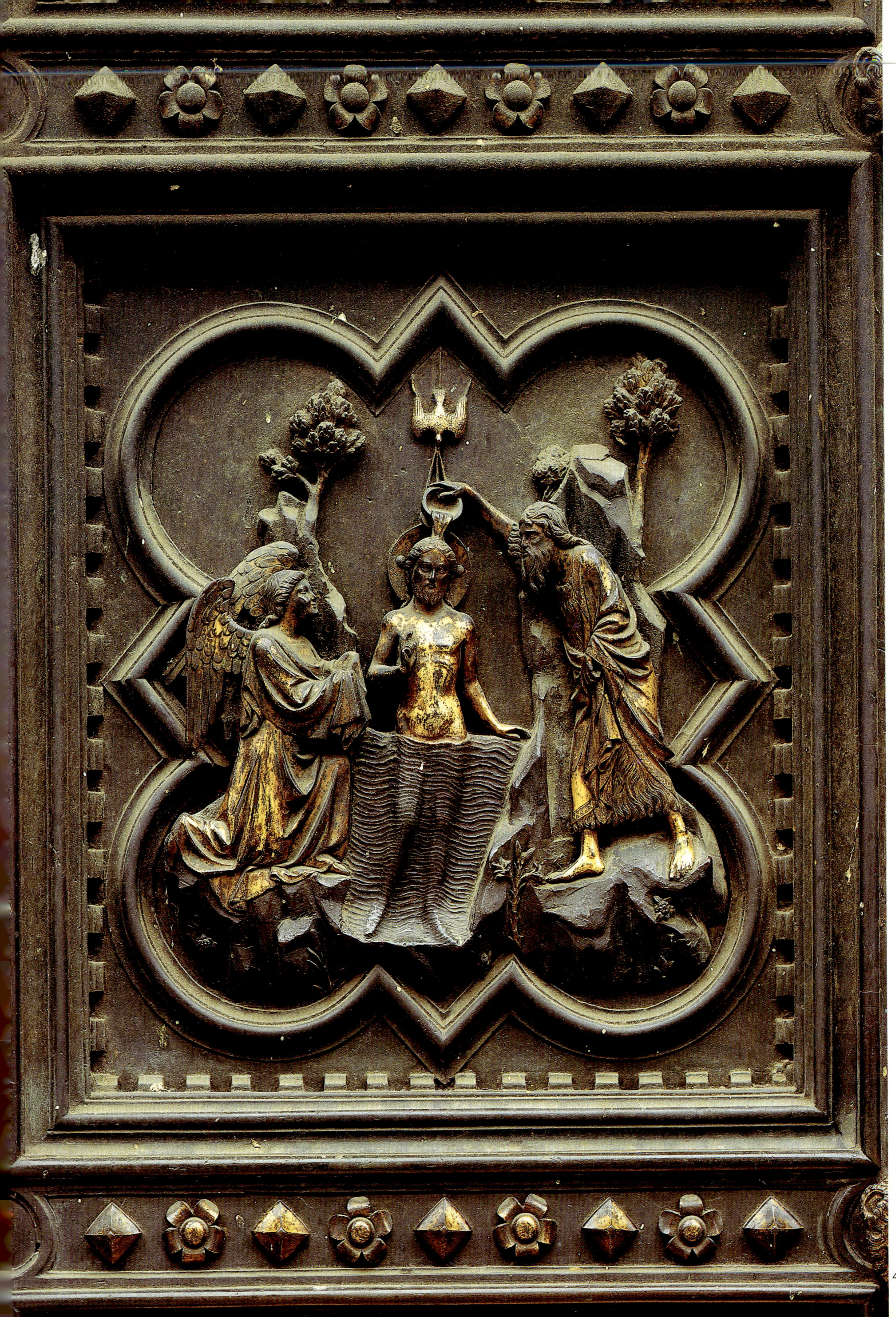

41.

42.
43. ▶

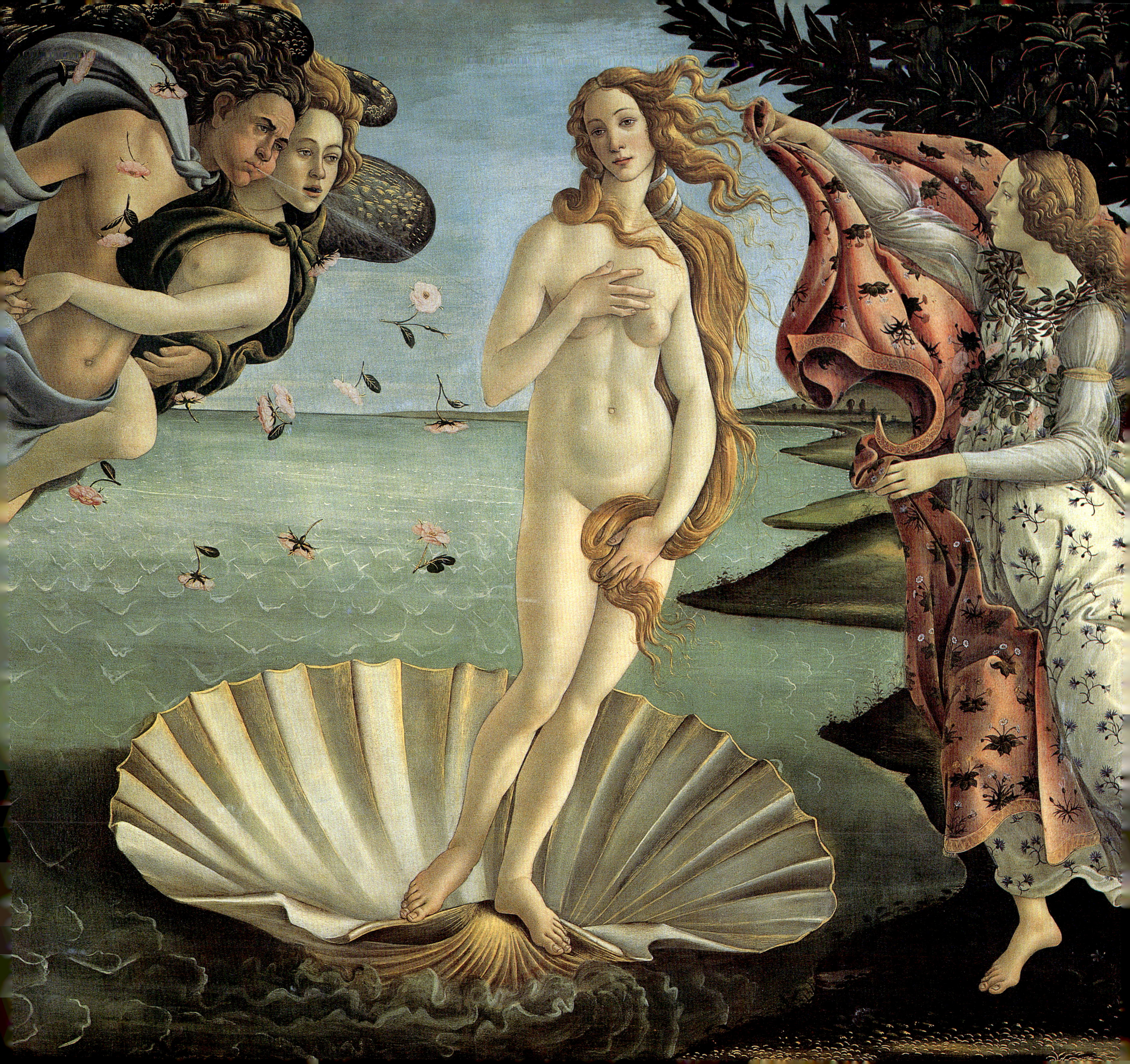

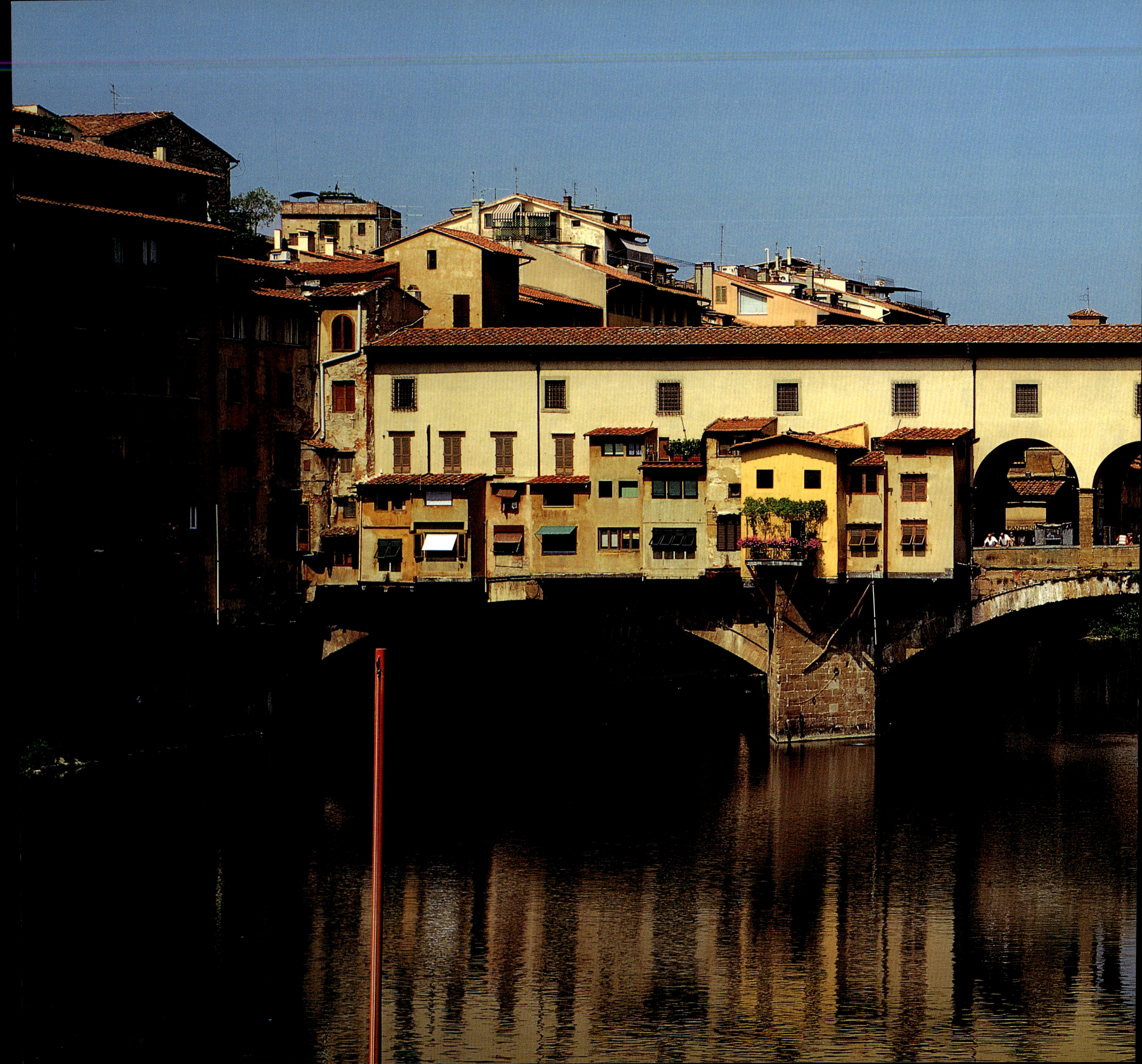

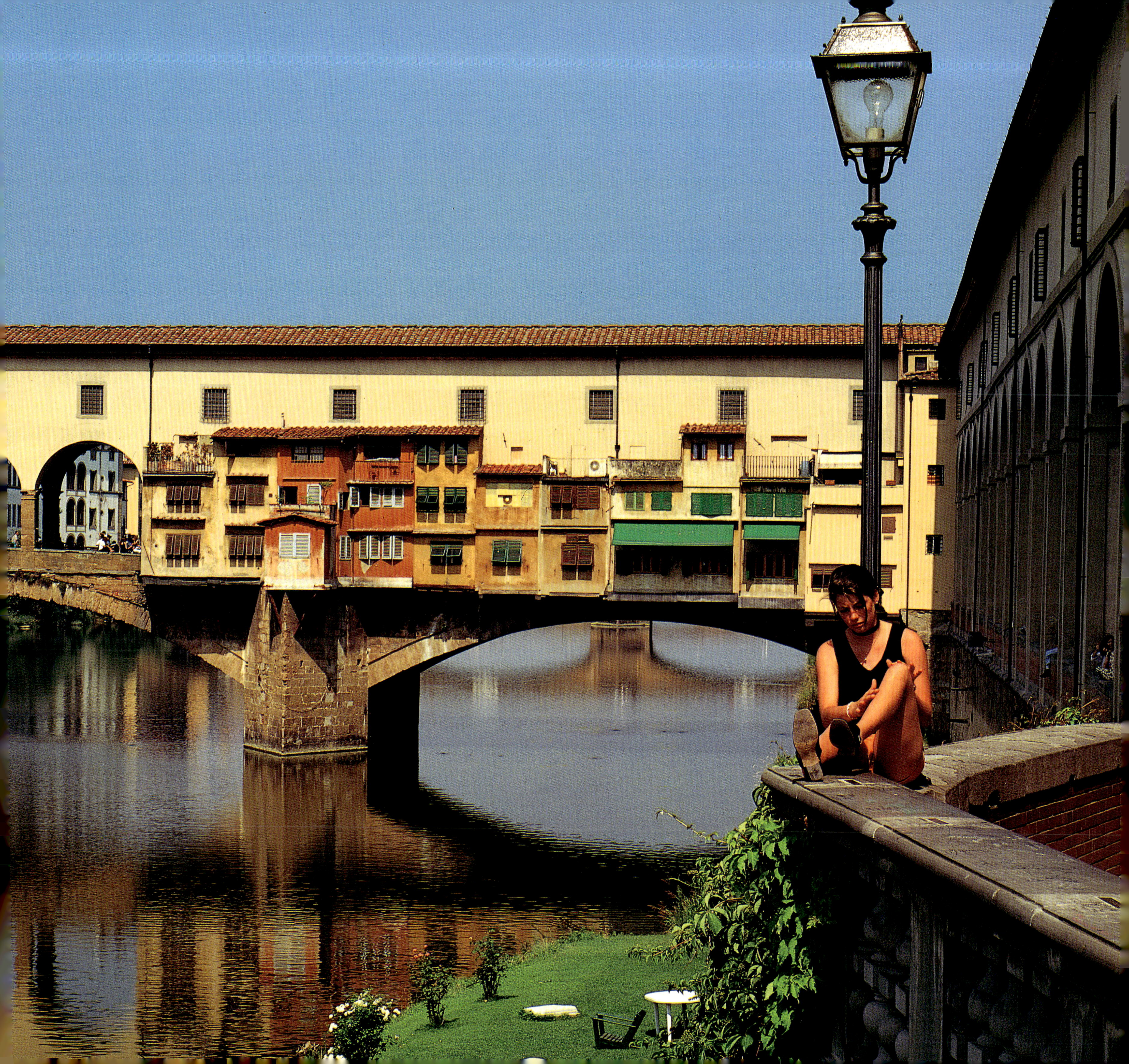

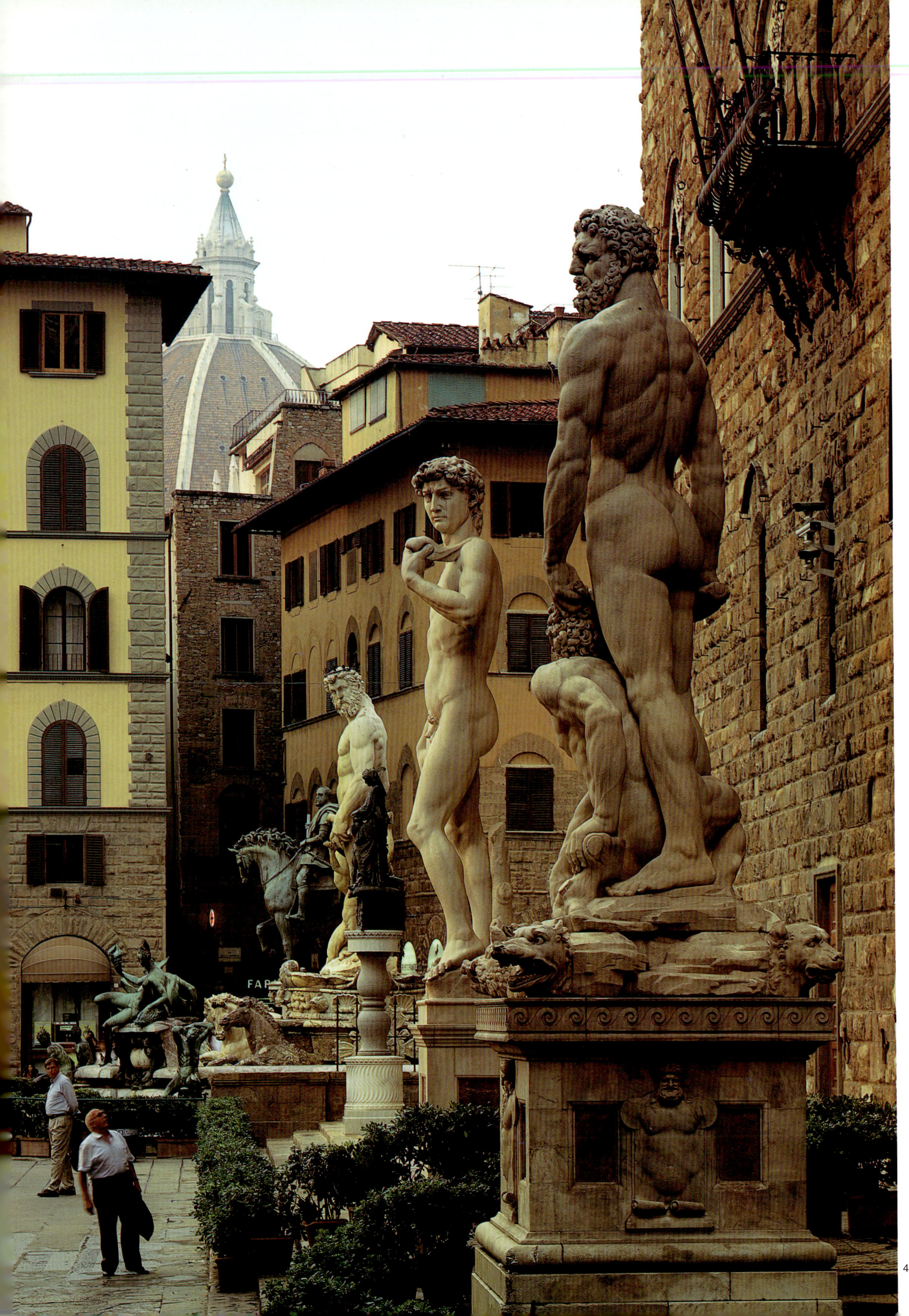

44.

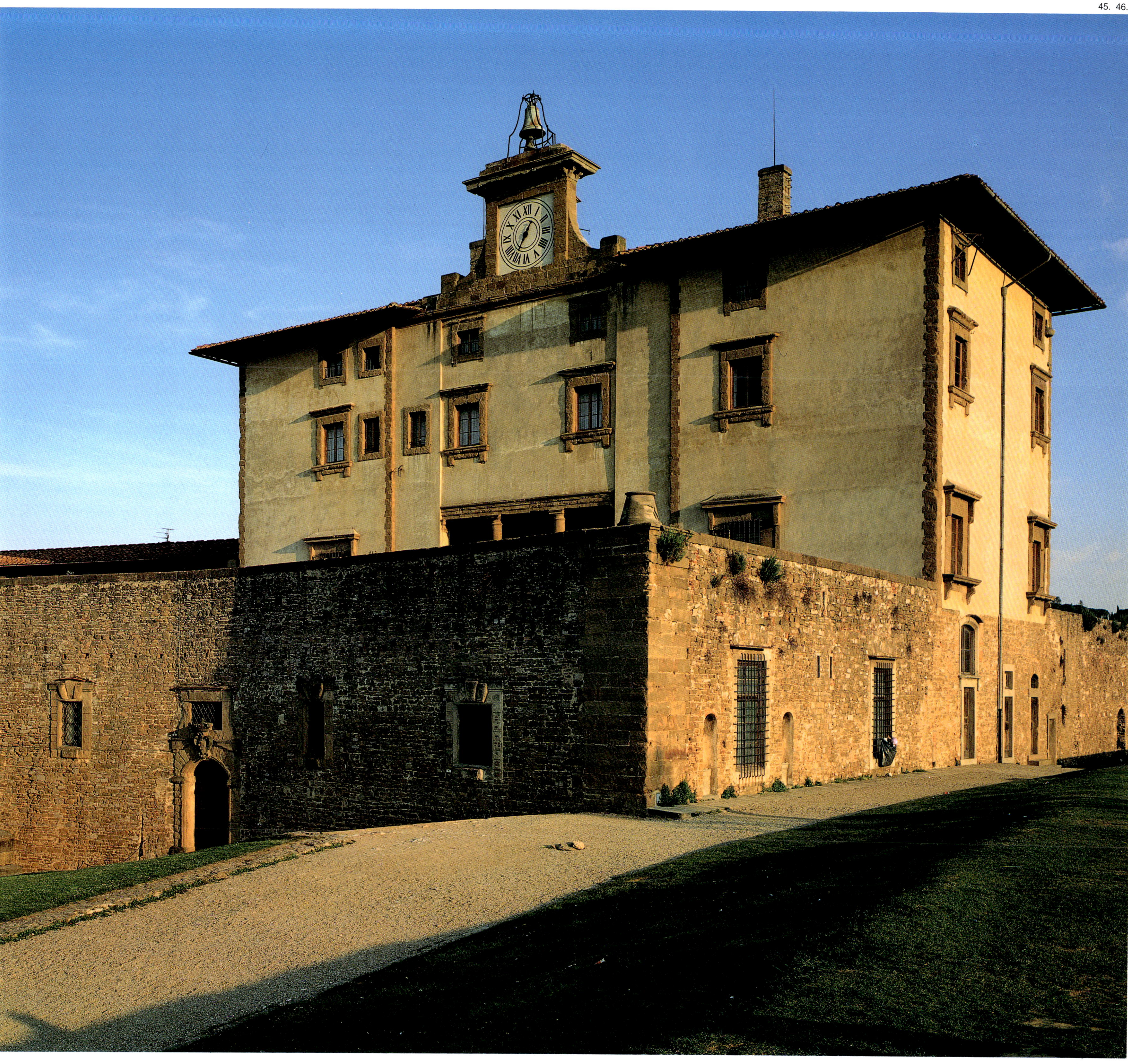

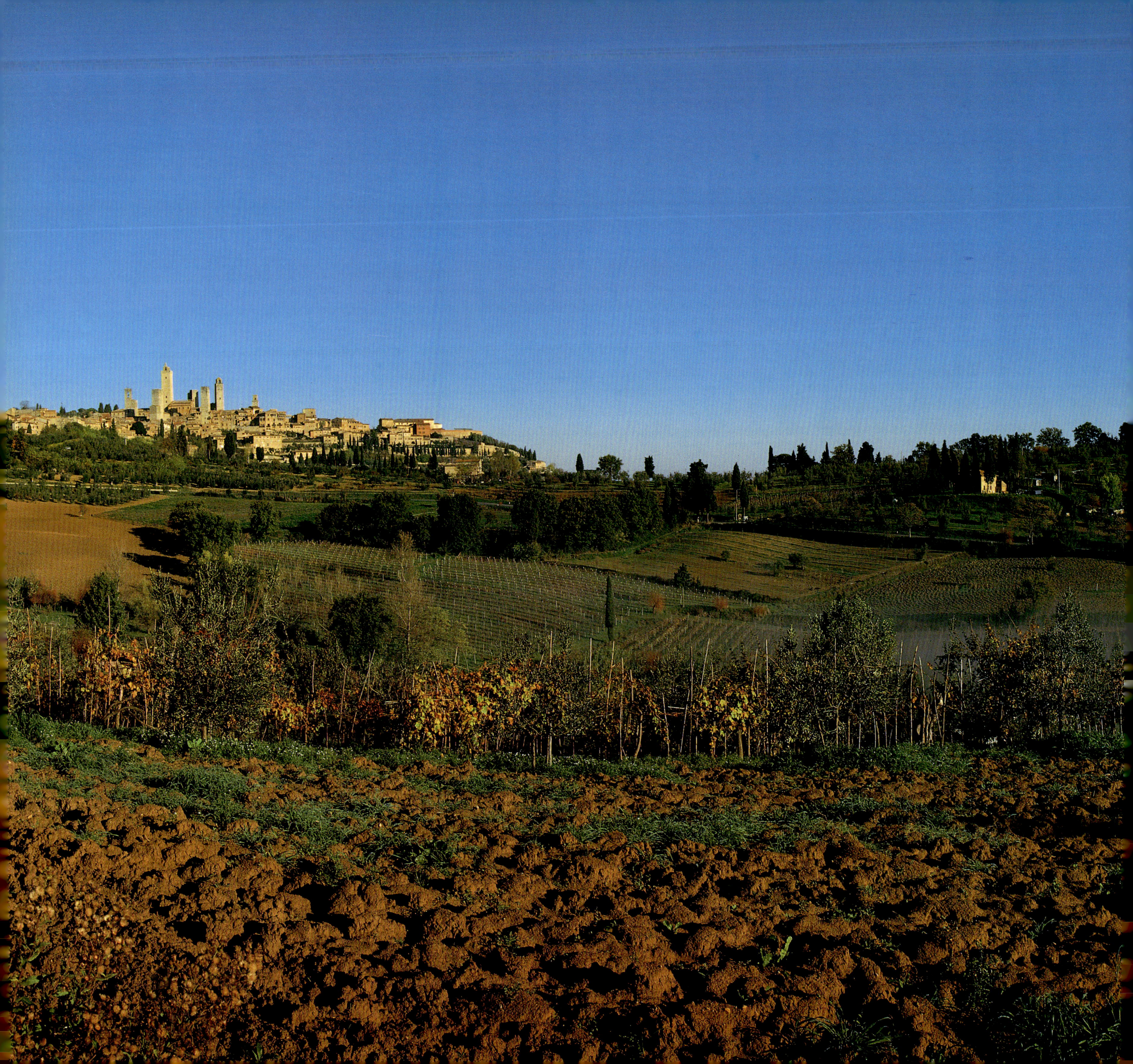

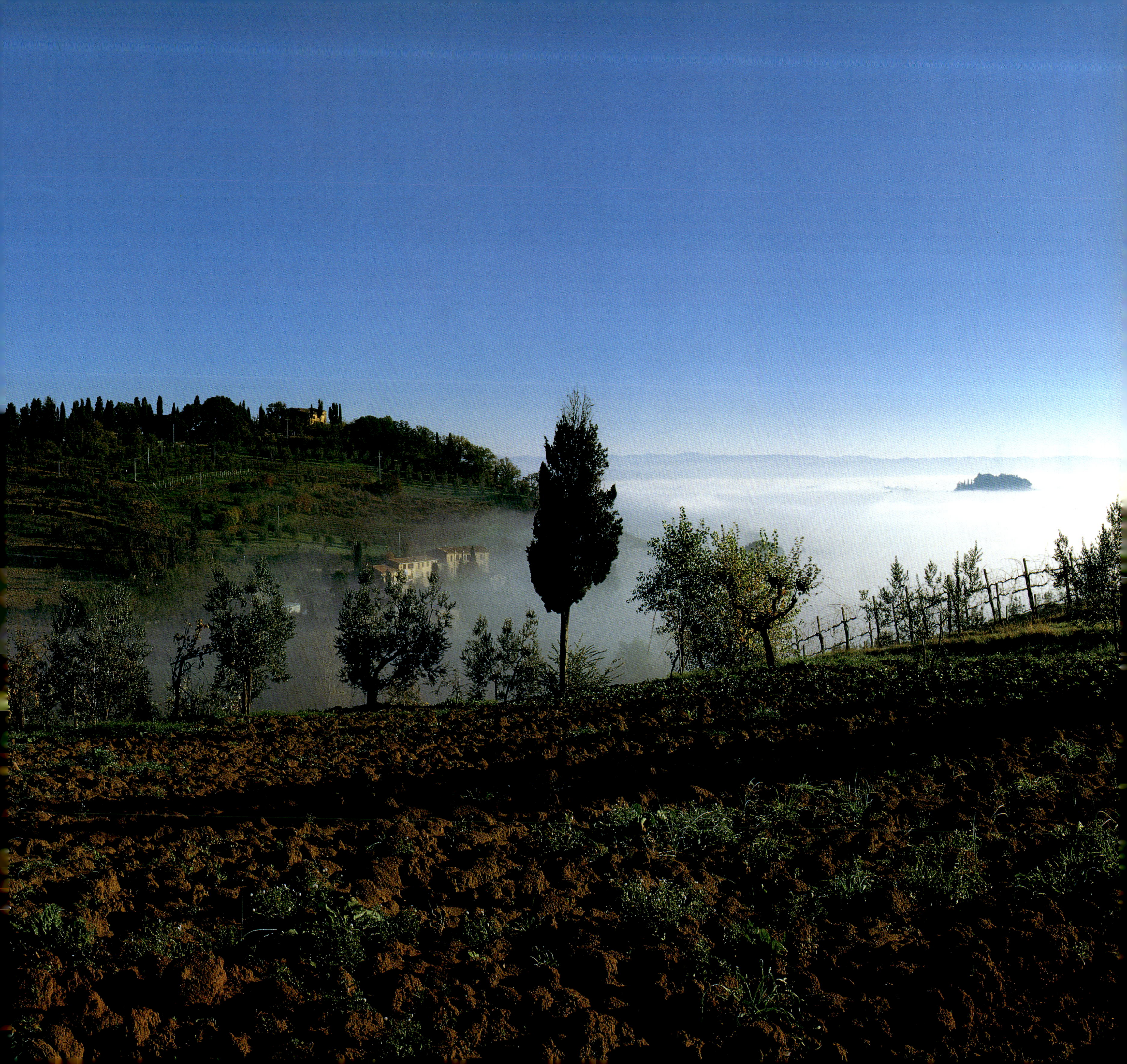

47.

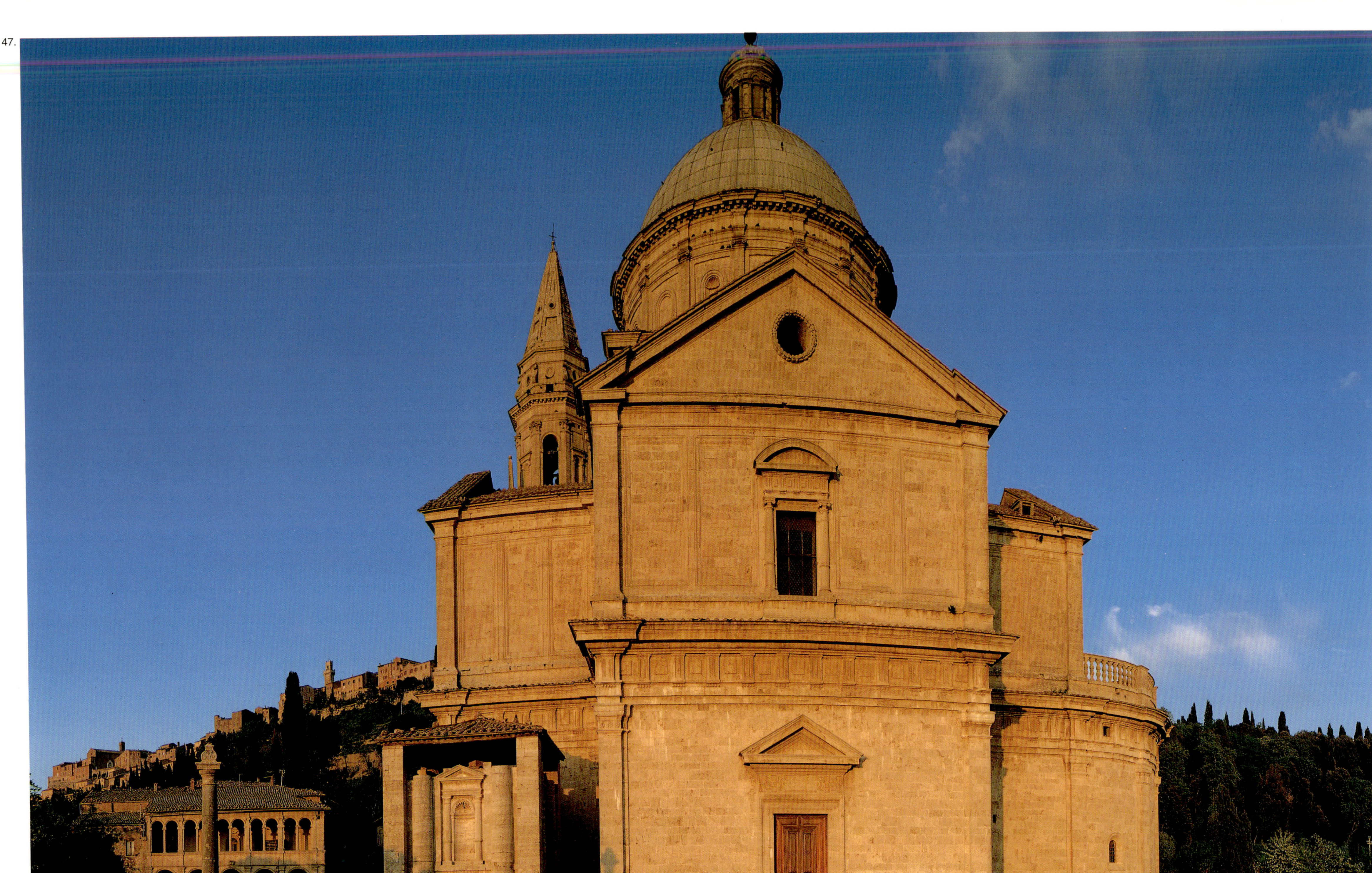

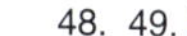
48. 49. ▶

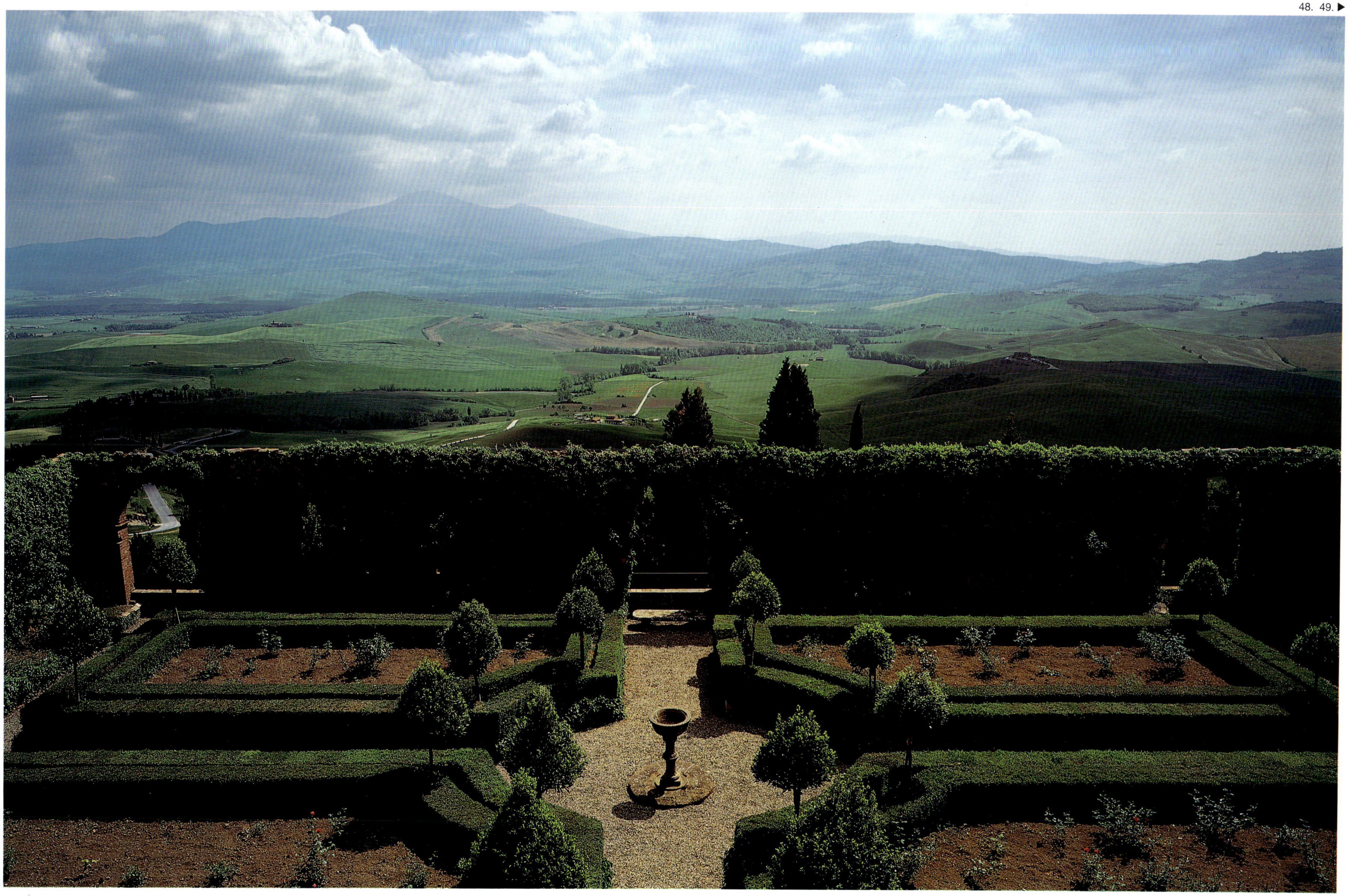

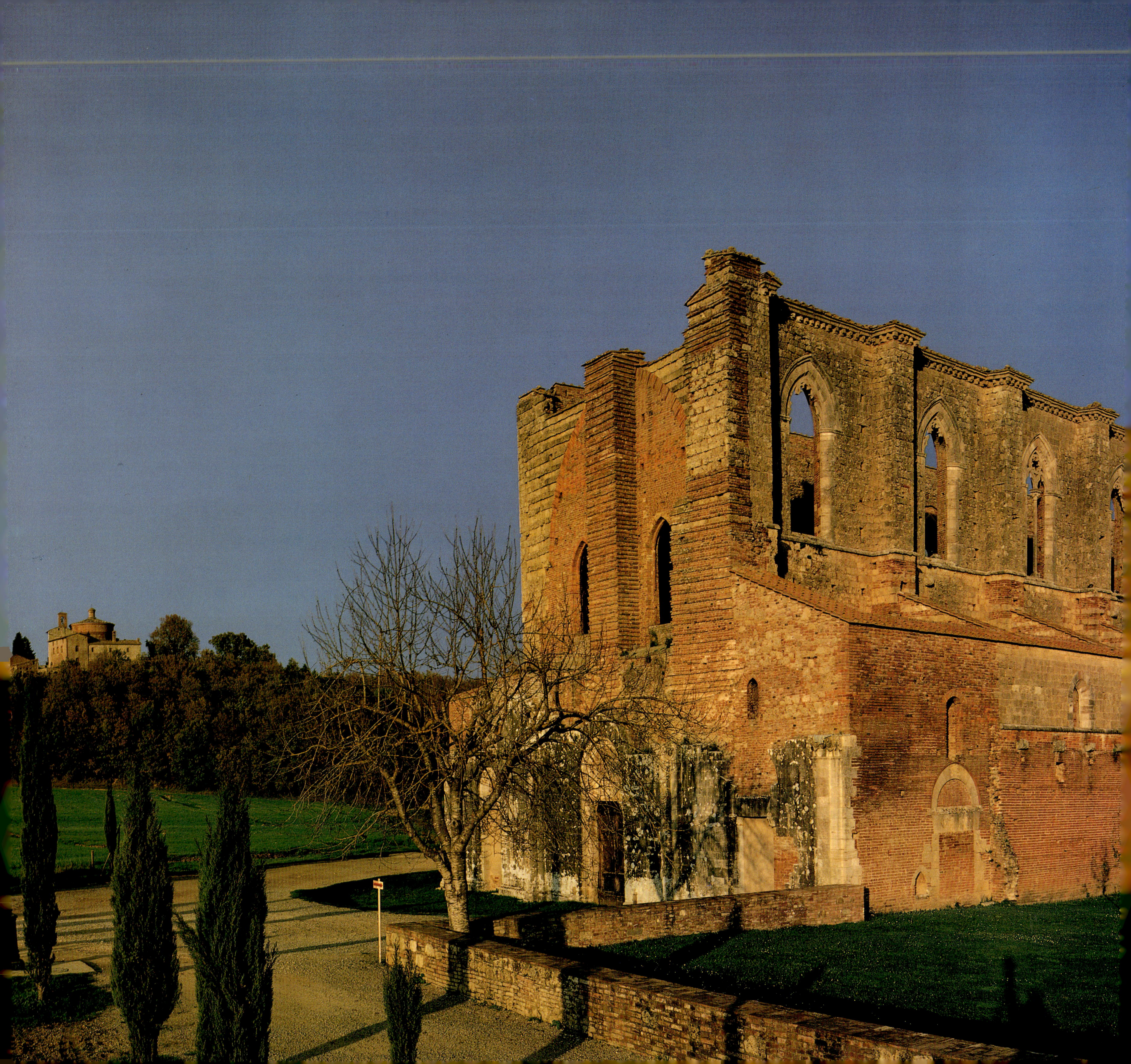

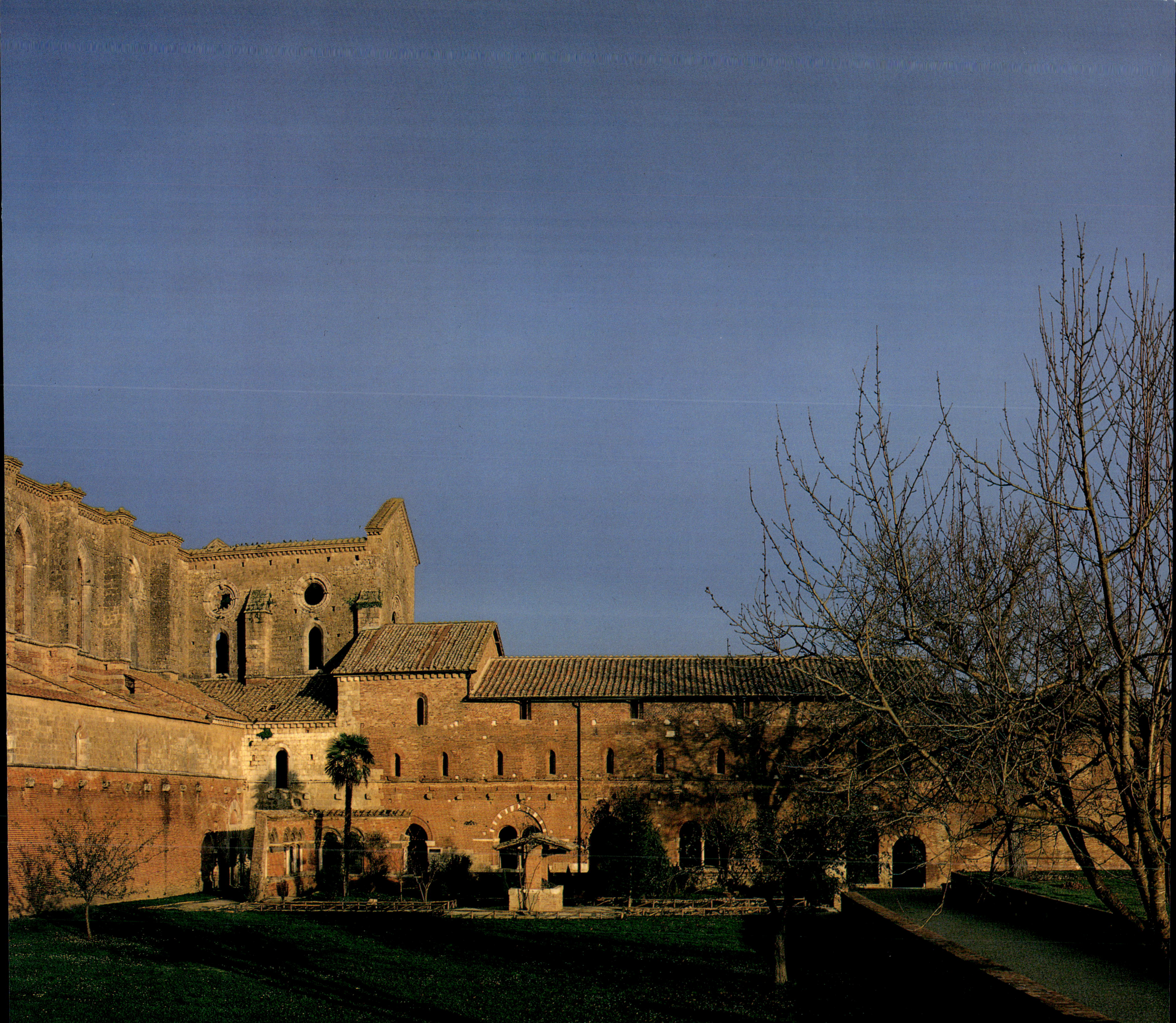

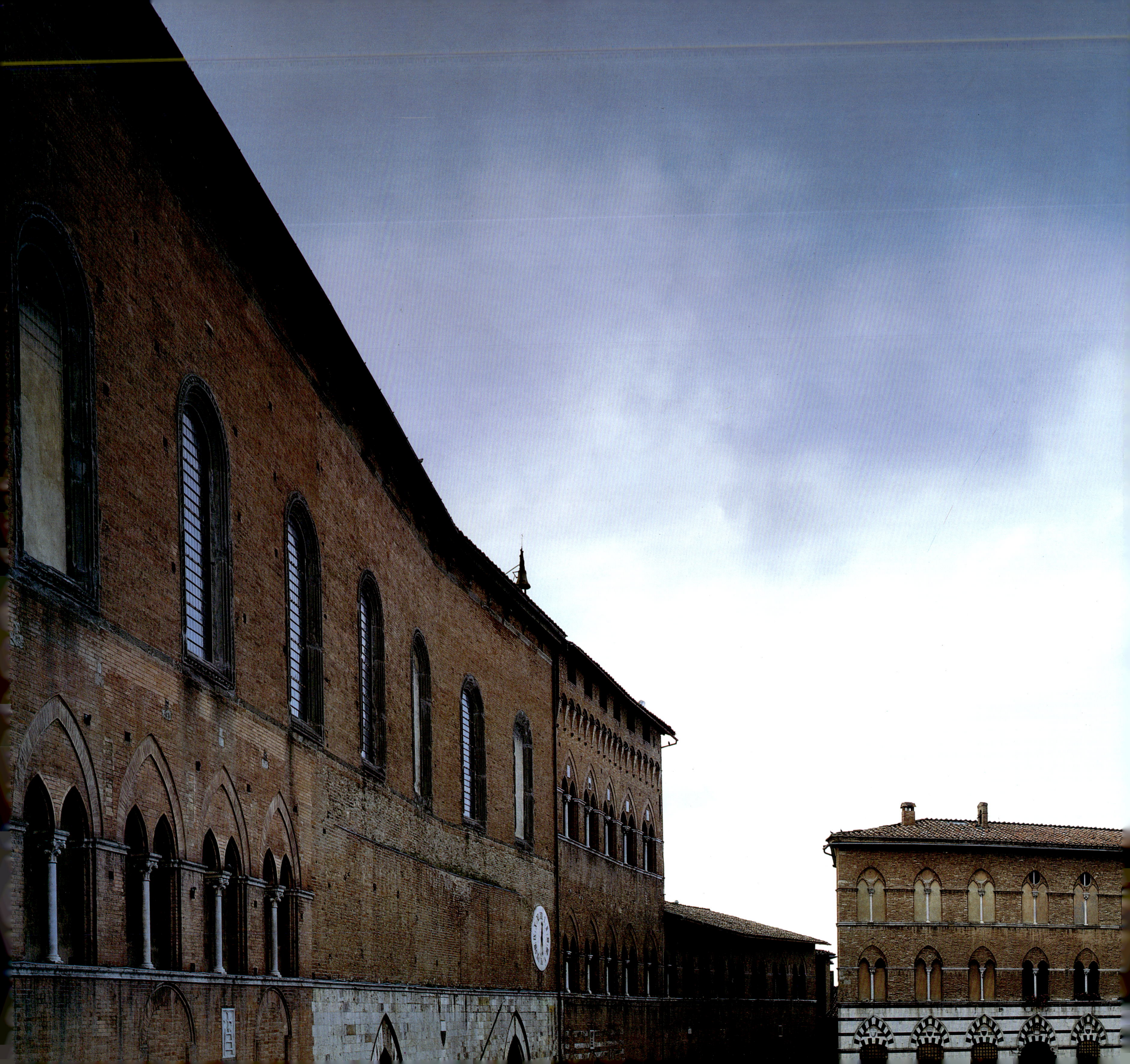

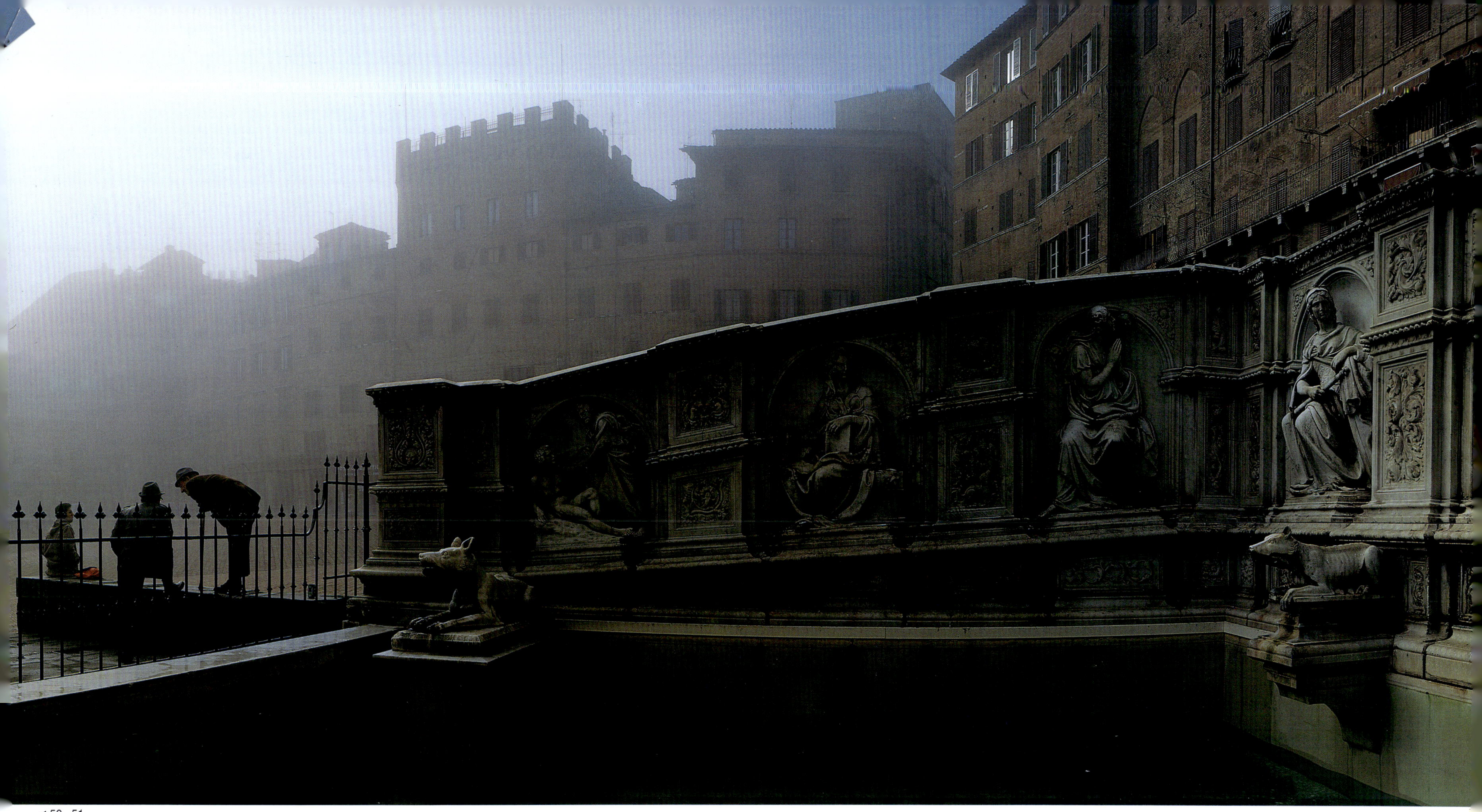

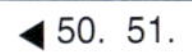 50. 51.

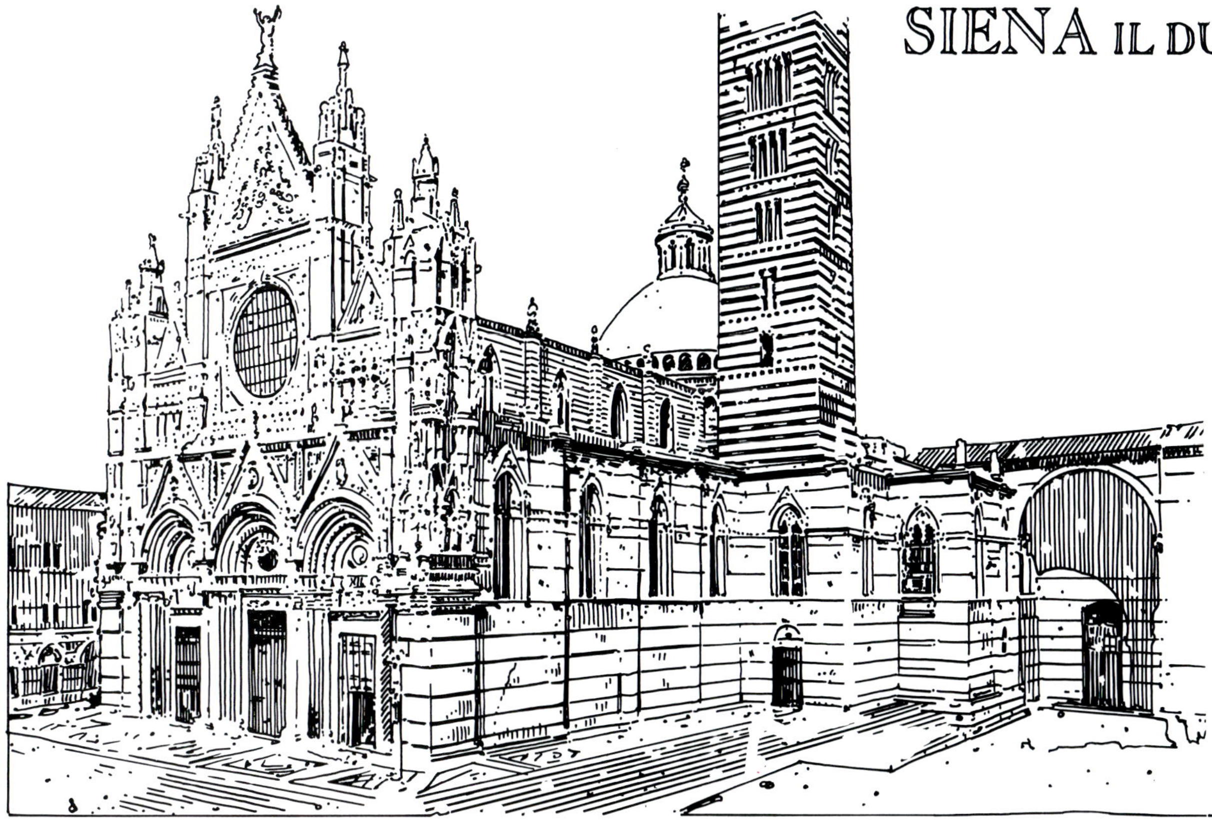

SIENA IL DUOMO

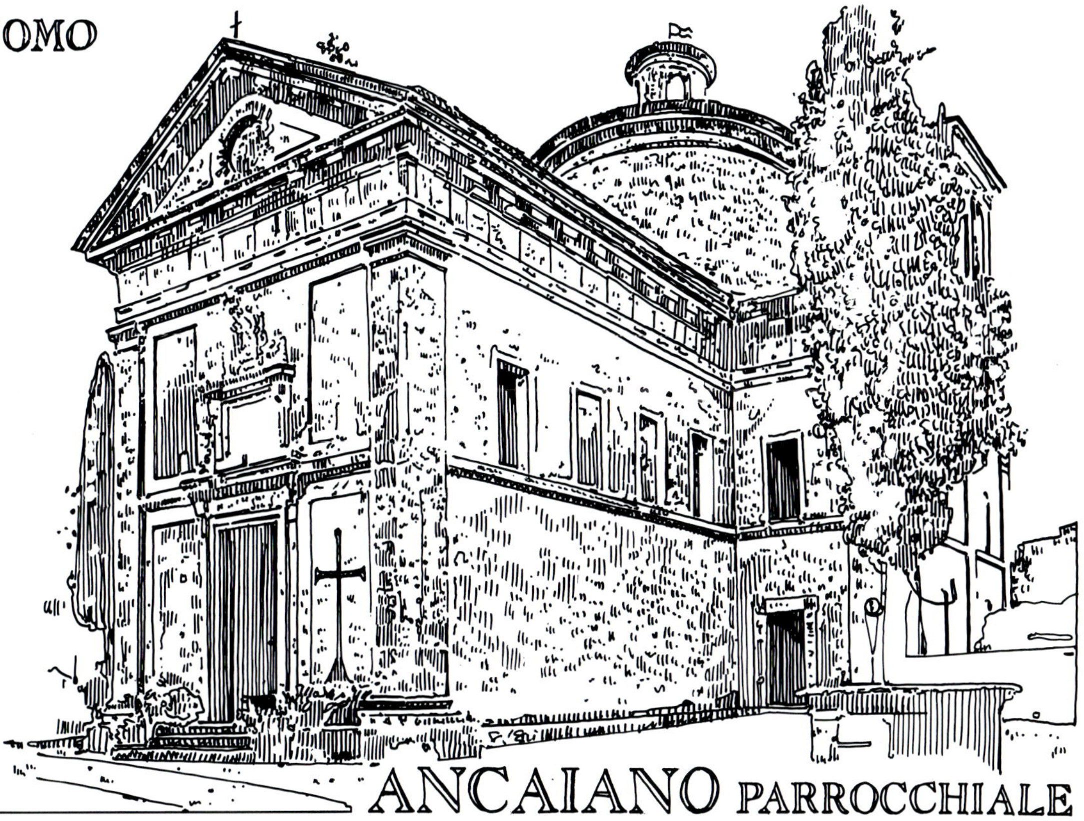

ANCAIANO PARROCCHIALE

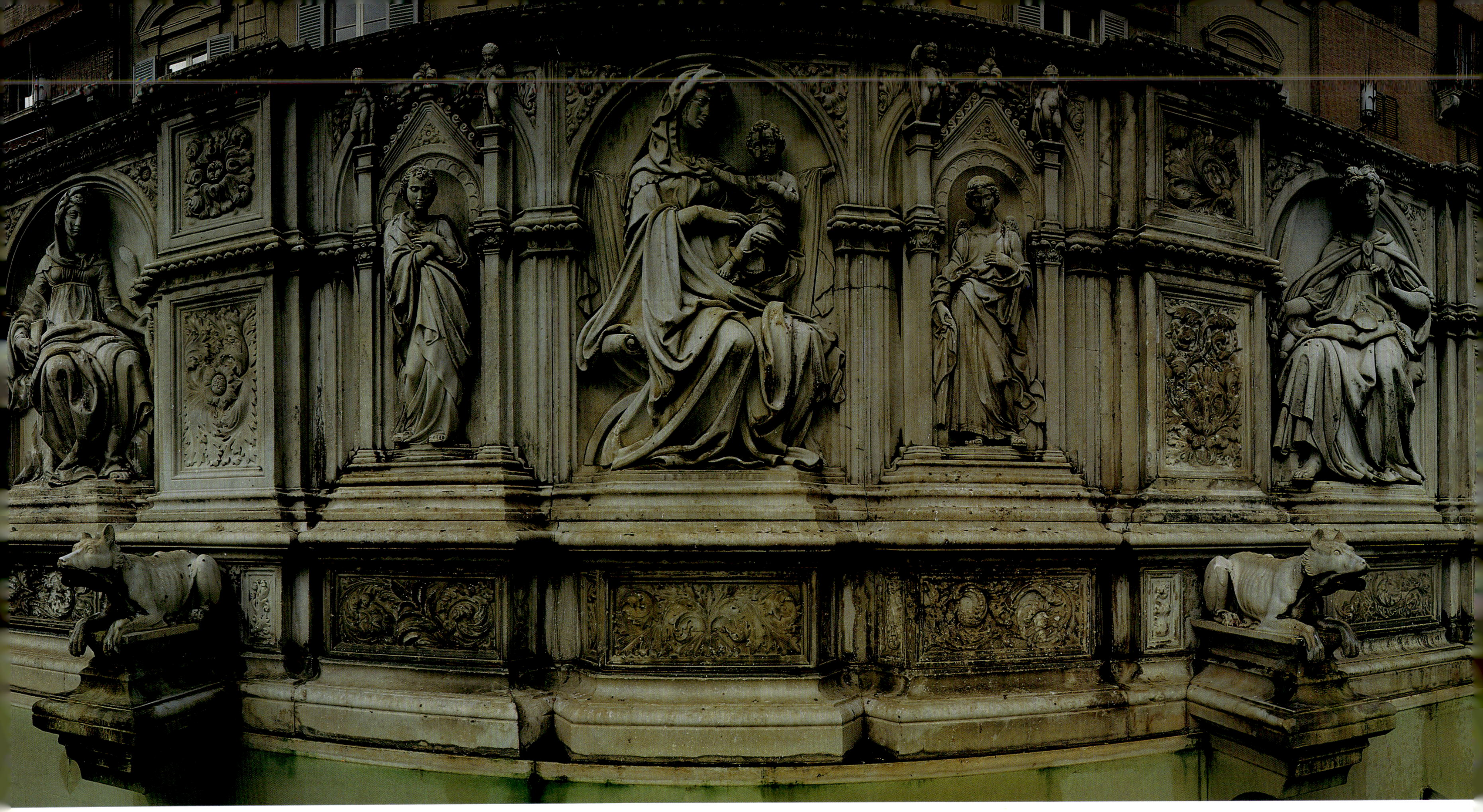

SAN GIMIGNANO
CORTILE DEL PALAZZO COMUNALE

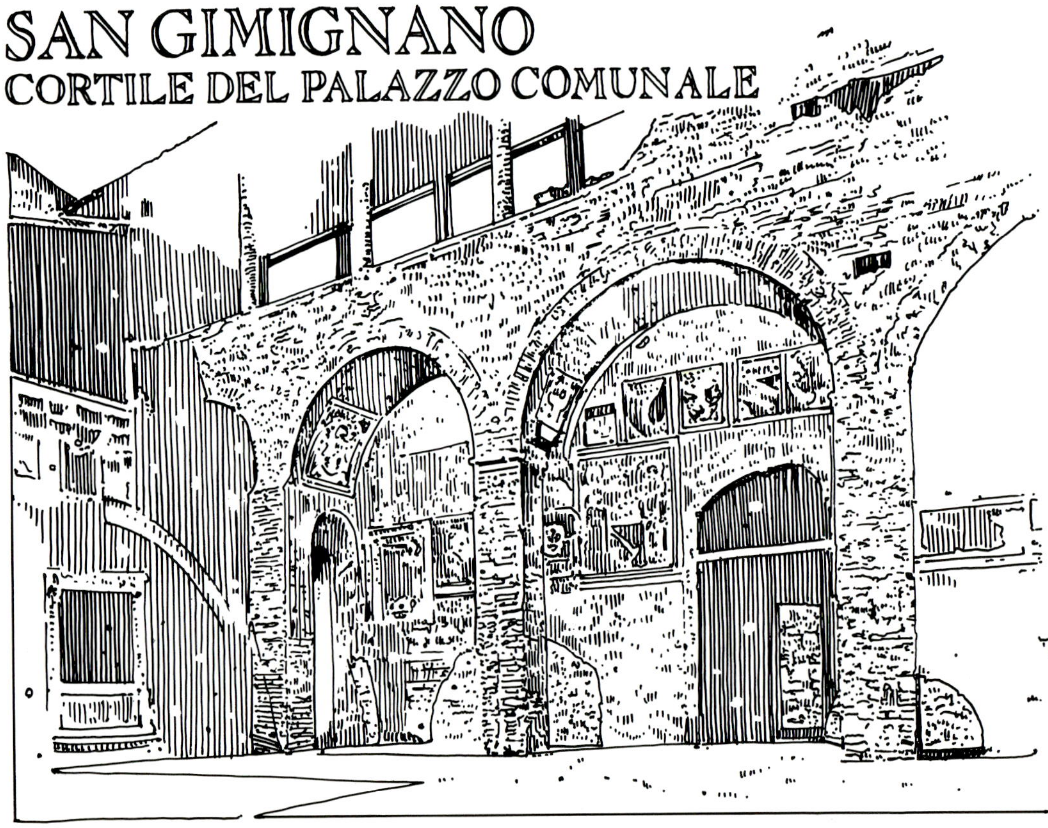

MONTALCINO
CHIESA DI S. AGOSTINO

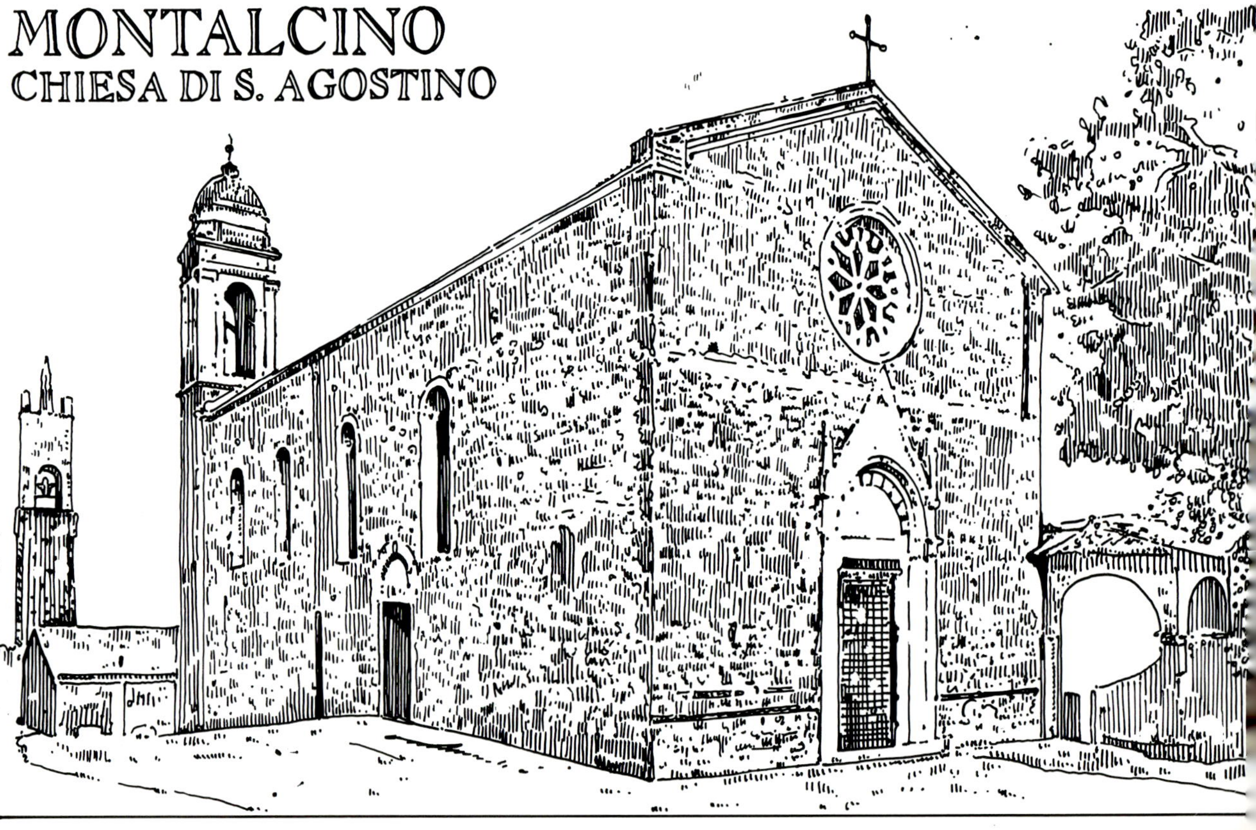

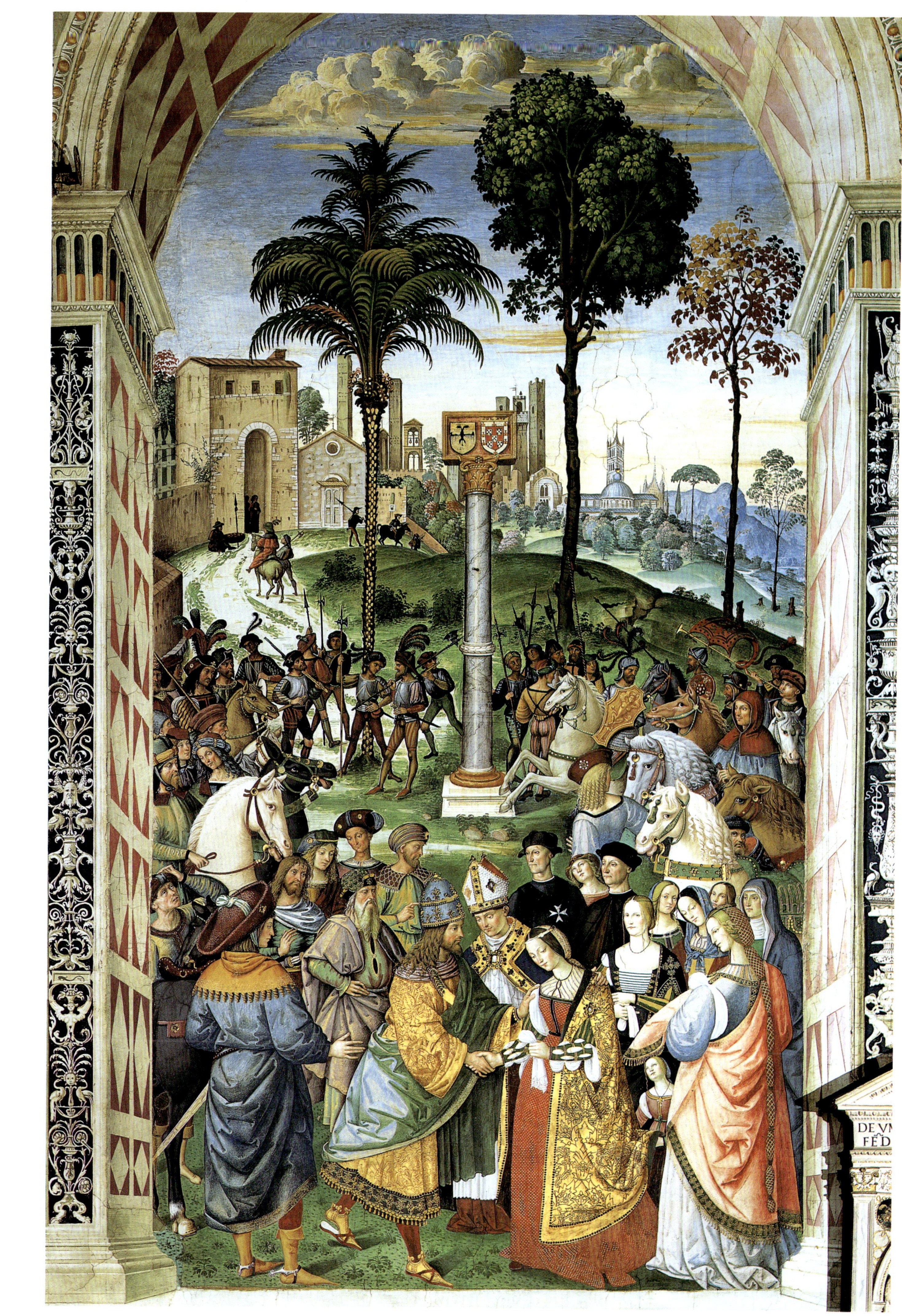
DE VN
FED

53.

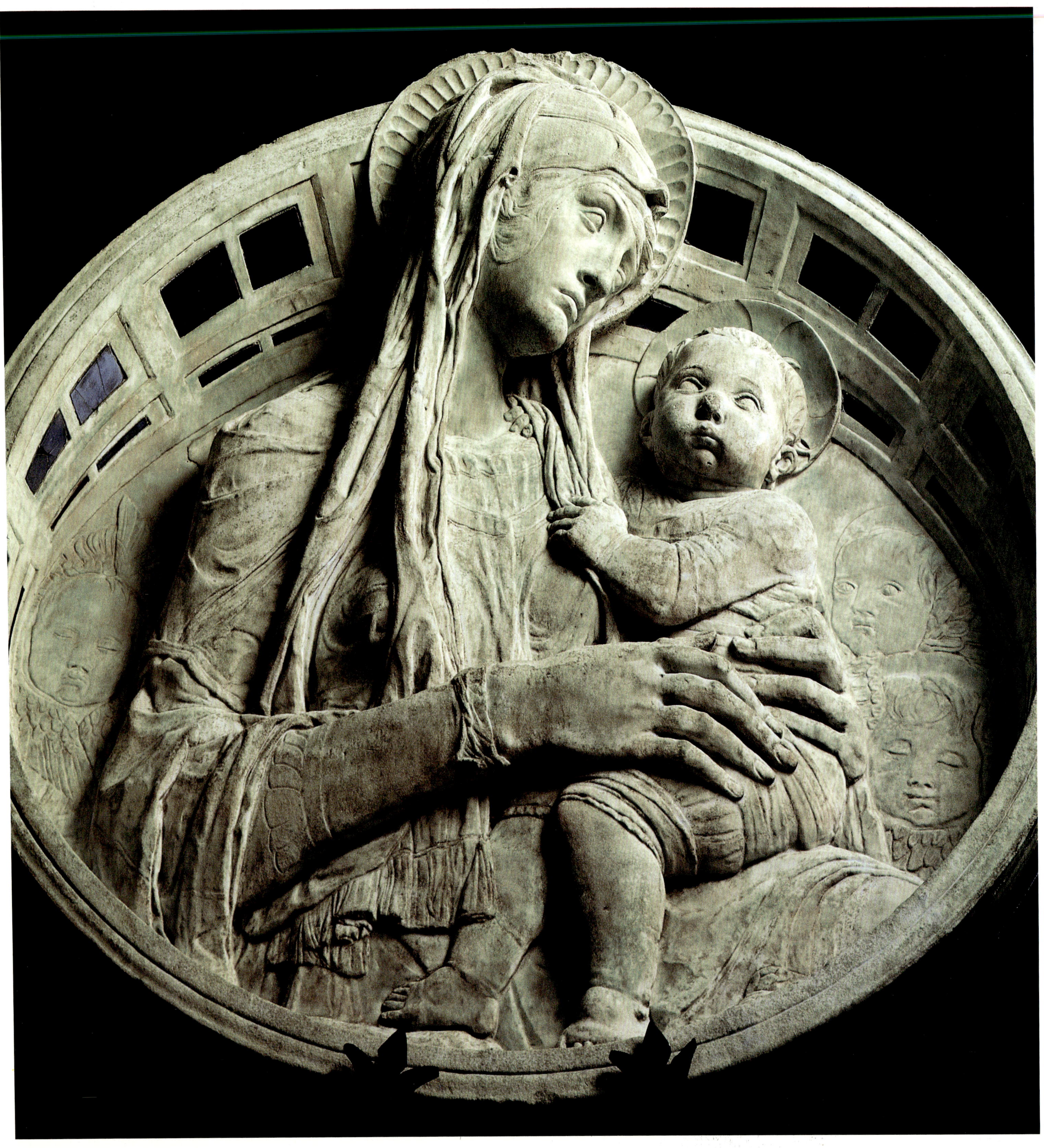

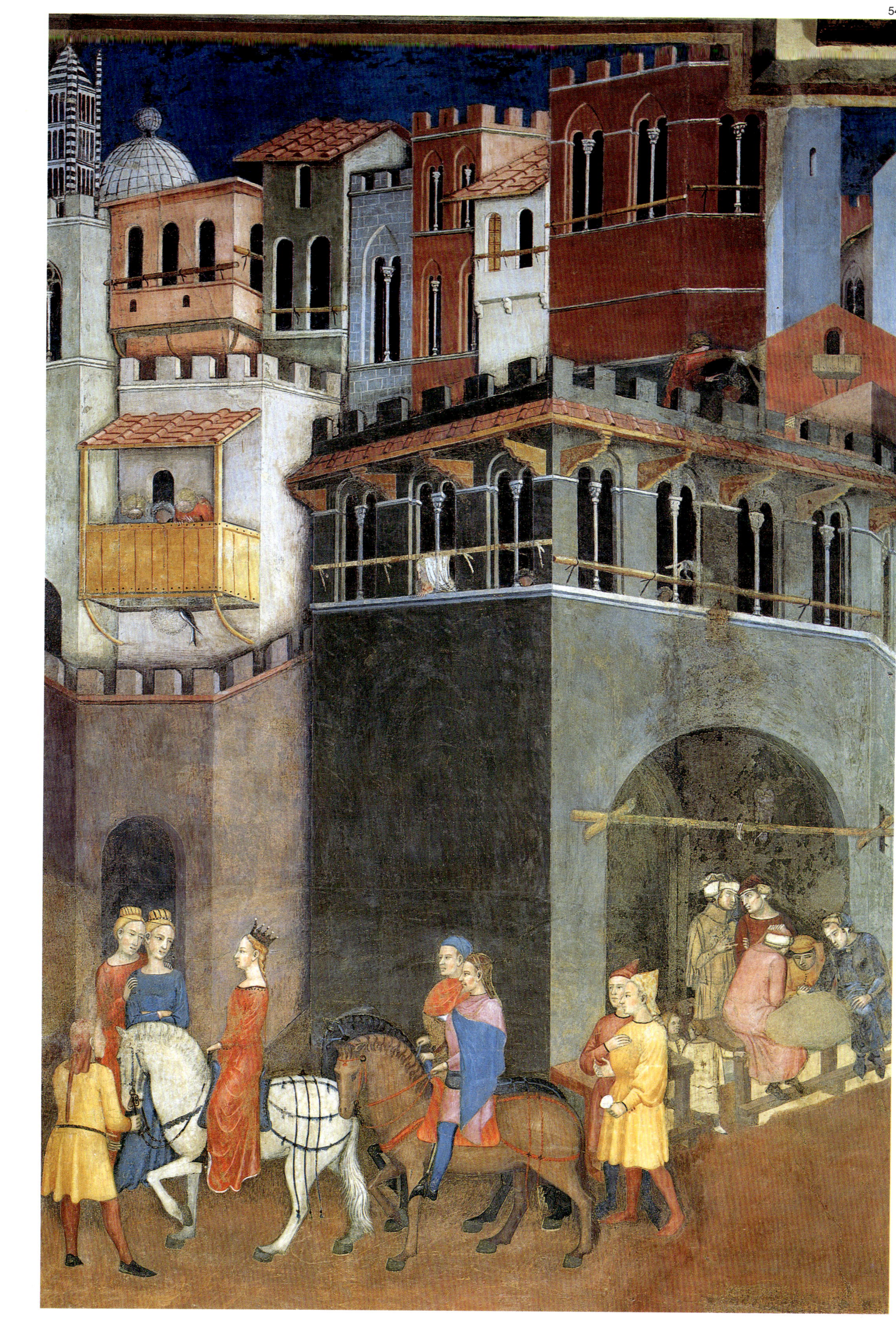

55.

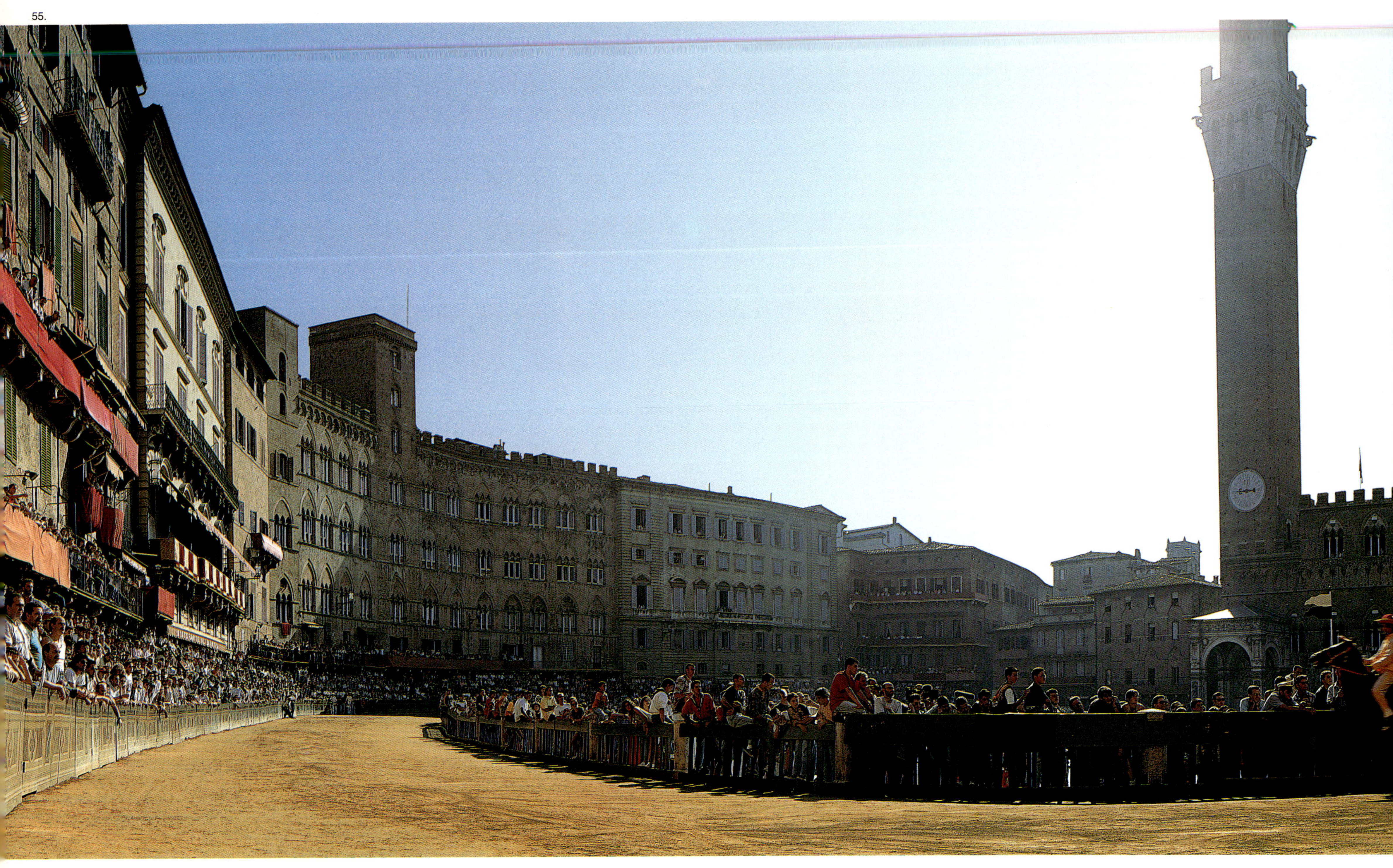

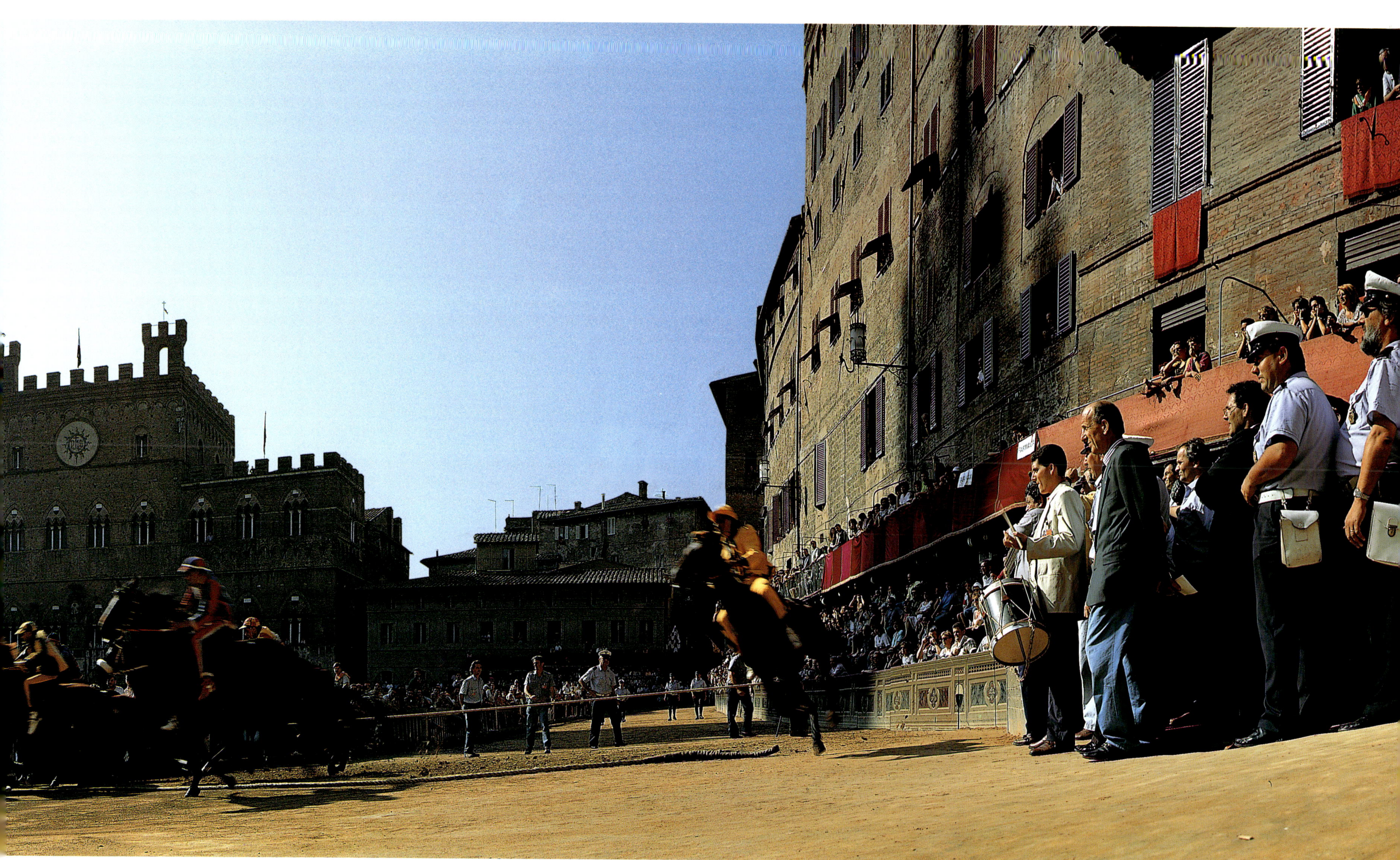

56.

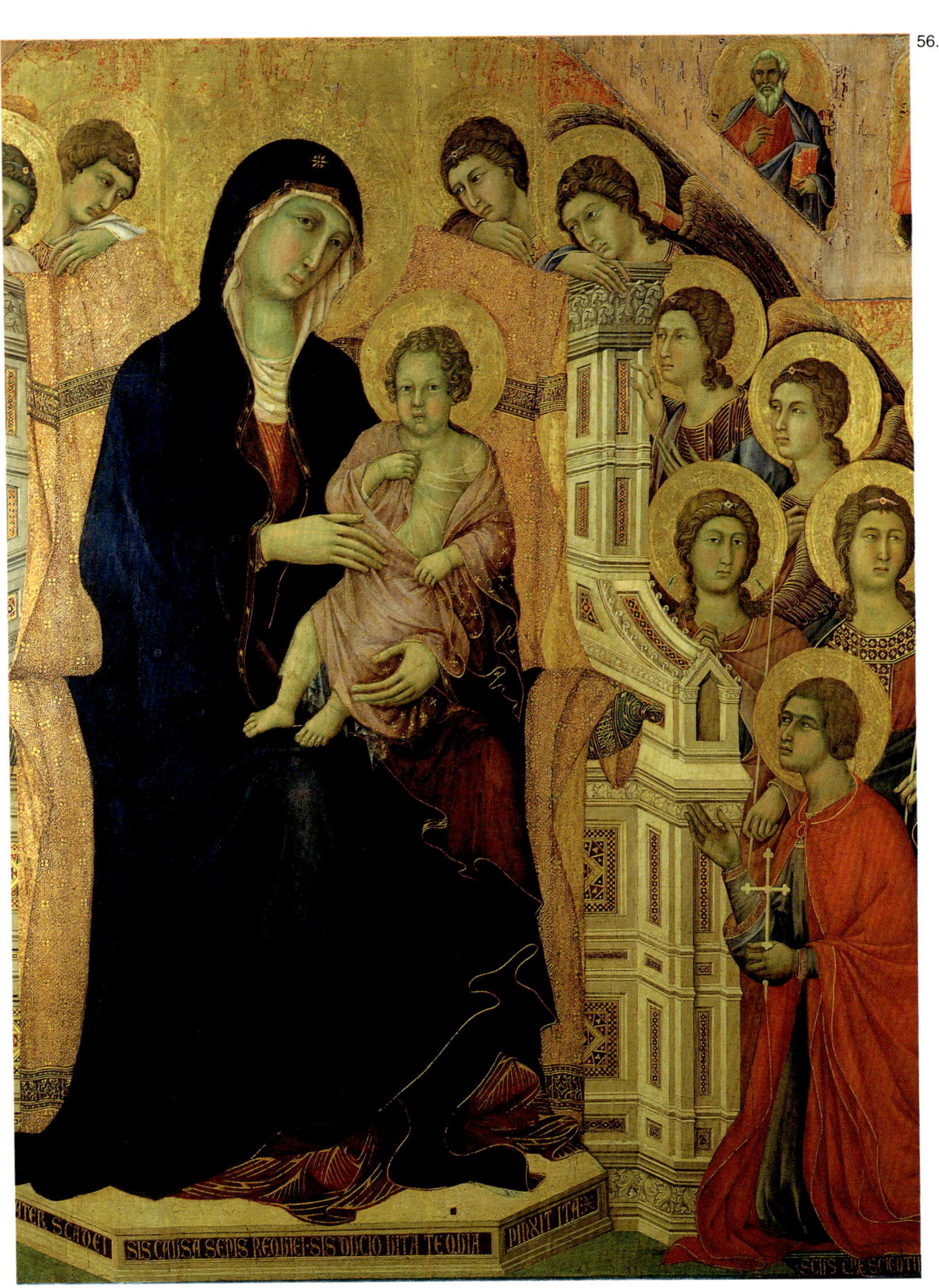

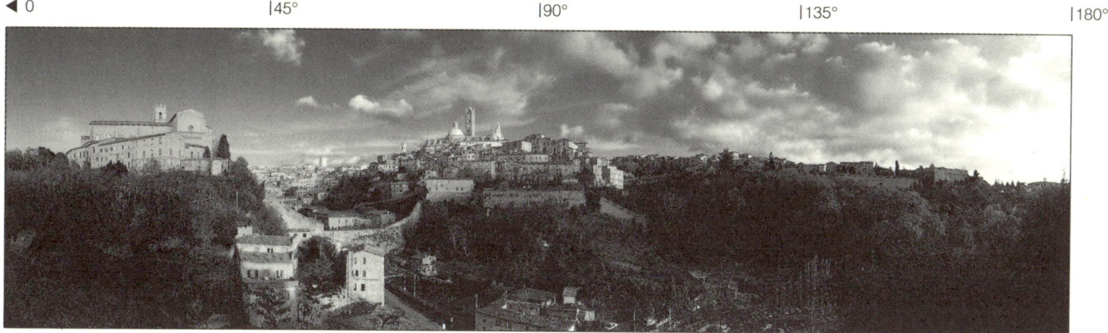

Cover: The white Duomo towers stand above Siena's clustered red houses and meandering streets. Below, sprawling to the right, is the Spedale di Santa Maria della Scala; to the left is the Basilica di San Domenico.

1.

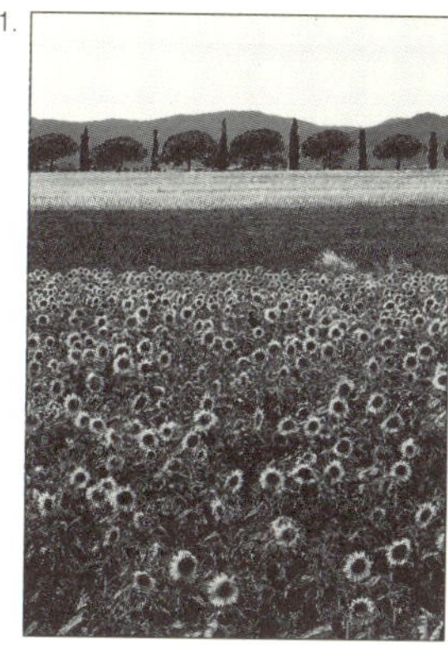

Maremma landscape with sunflowers and a row of trees—cypress alternating with round maritime pine.

2.

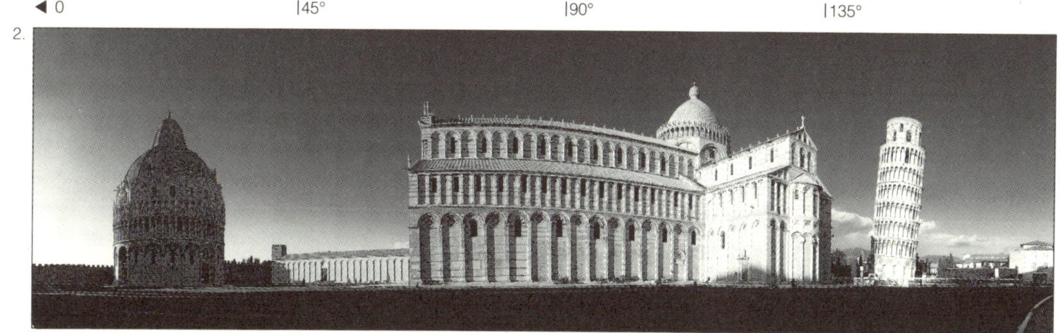

Pisa: Buscheto began work on this cathedral in 1064; Rainaldo completed the apse and façade near the end of the thirteenth century. To the right, the leaning tower of Pisa.

3.

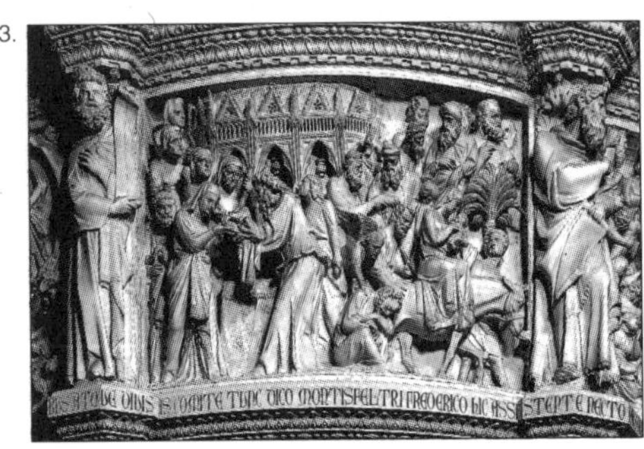

A pulpit by Giovanni Pisano, early fourteenth century. The pulpit was dismantled around 1599 and reassembled in 1926. The scenes shown here are the presentation of the infant Jesus in the Temple and the flight into Egypt.

4.

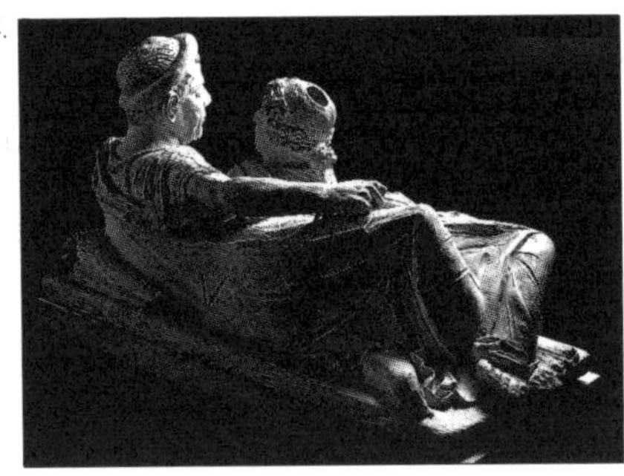

In the Museo Guarnacci, Volterra: husband and wife, an example of the Etruscan sculpture work for cinerary urns and caskets.

5.

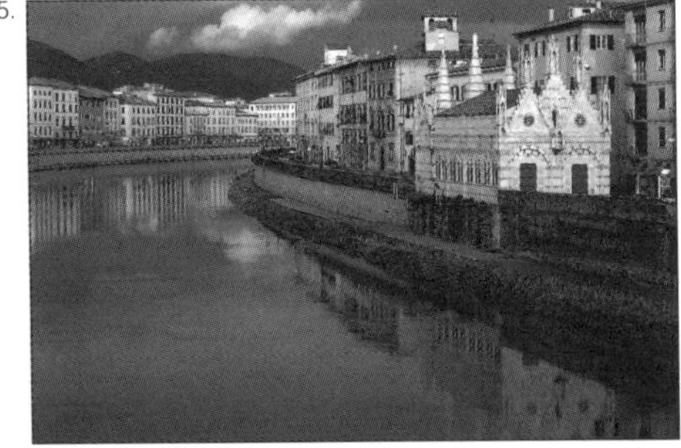

A view of Pisa and the Lung'Arno waterway. To the right is the church of Santa Maria della Spina, which takes its name from a relic kept there of Christ's crown of thorns. The church also holds sculptures by Tommaso Pisano and Giovanni di Balduccio.

6.

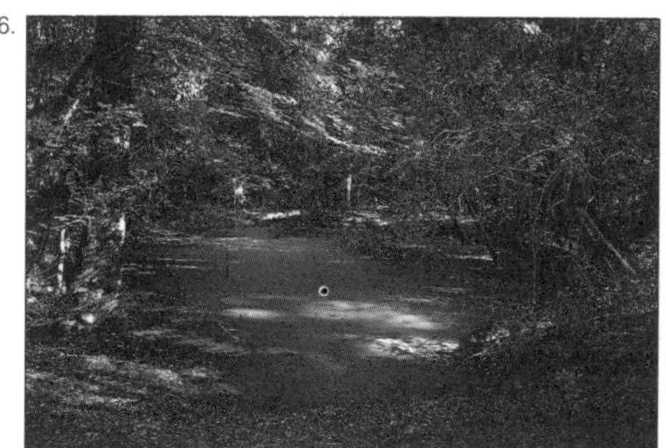

A swamp in the area bounded by the mouths of the Arno and the Serchio, which is one of the few stretches of the Tyrrhenian coastal forest to remain intact. It is home to wildlife ranging from wild boar to deer to many varieties of birds and thick woods of oak and pine.

◀ 0 |45° |90° |135°

7.

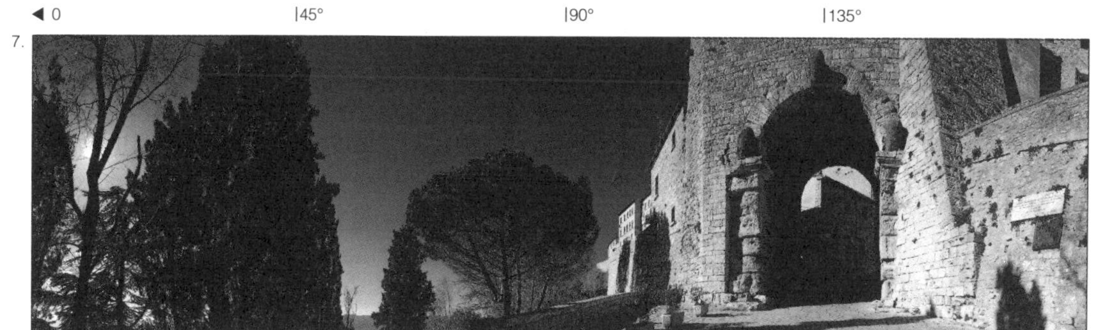

The hill of Volterra, less than twenty miles from the sea, has been inhabited since neolithic times. After the Villanovan civilization, which lasted until the seventh century B.C.E., the Etruscan city Velathri was founded here. It profited from iron and alabaster excavations, and its merchants traded their products throughout the Mediterranean. The city walls date from this period. The Etruscan Arch, or Porta dell'Arco, shown here, was then the city's busiest gate. In 1944 the citizens fiercely defended it from the invading Germans.

8.

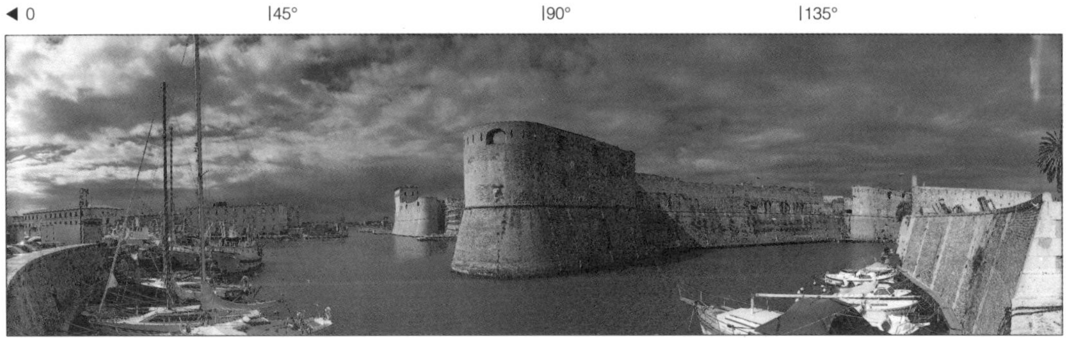

A view of the watchtower Mastio di Matilde, the Fortezza Vecchia, and the city of Livorno. Beneath its walls, to the south, lies the Darsena Vecchia, the harbor from which Amerigo Vespucci set sail on oceanic explorations.

9.

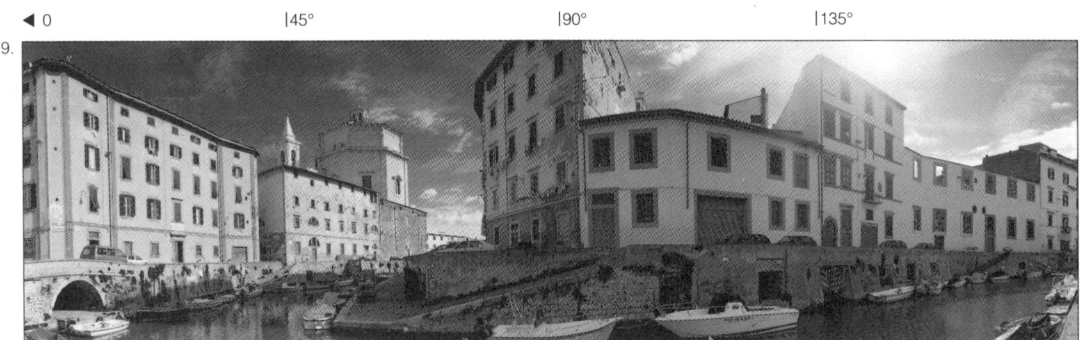

Livorno was inaugurated in 1577 by Bernardo Buontalenti, for Francesco de' Medici I, to replace the Port of Pisa. Venetian builders were brought in for their expertise in constructing over water, and Livorno was nicknamed "New Venice." Here, *palazzi* in the traditional Venetian style—residential apartments on the upper floors and stores on the lower level, with direct access to the water—overlook the Fosso Venezia waterway. In the center, the church of Santa Caterina.

10.

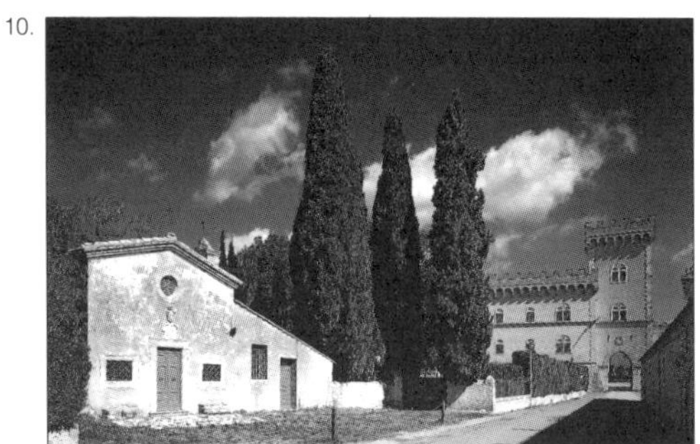

Bòlgheri.

11.

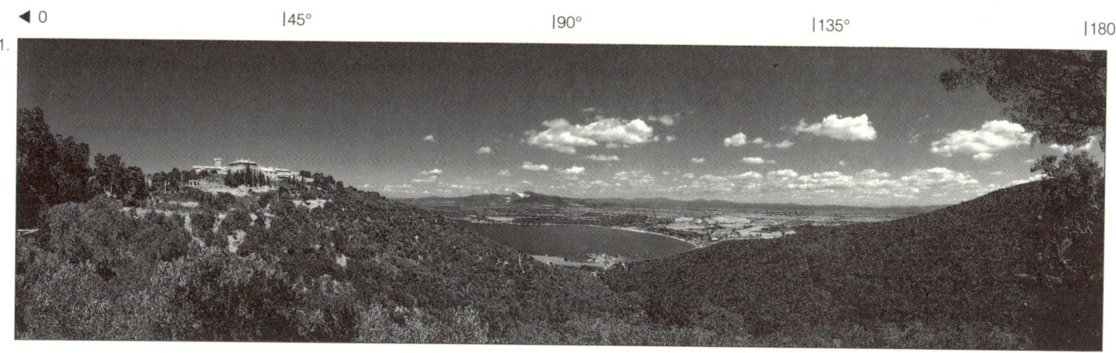

Populonia and the gulf of Baratti. This is an area with a strong history of metal working—from Villanovan copper mines to ninth-century-B.C.E. silver and tin work to Iron Age foundries. Three thousand years after the last, during World War I, Populonia was once again sought out for its ore.

12.

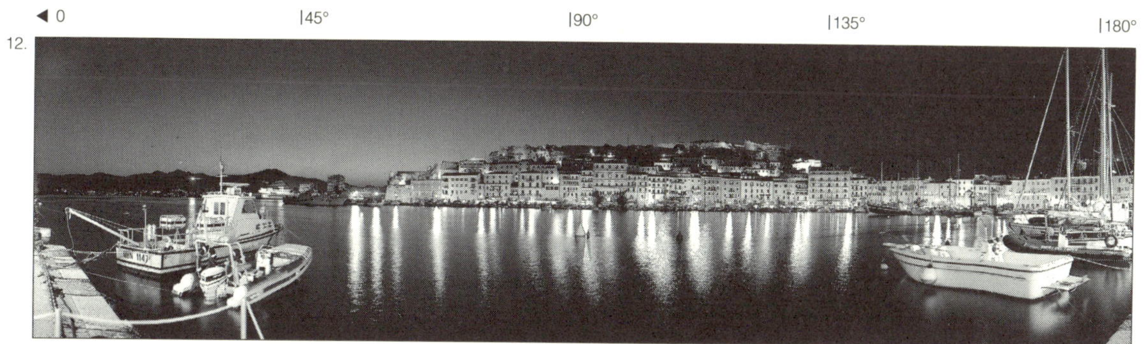

Portoferraio, Elba, by night.

13.

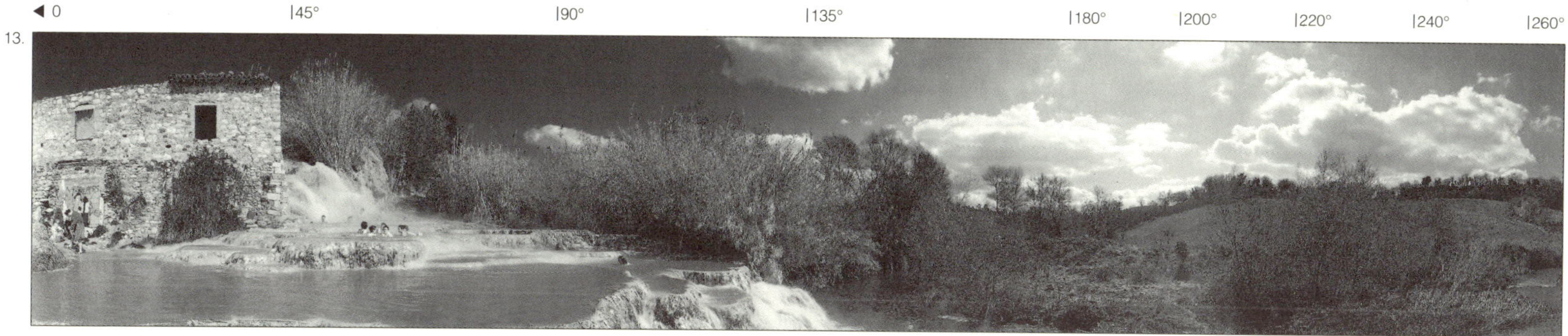

The sulfur falls, therapeutic spring waters, outside Saturnia.

14.

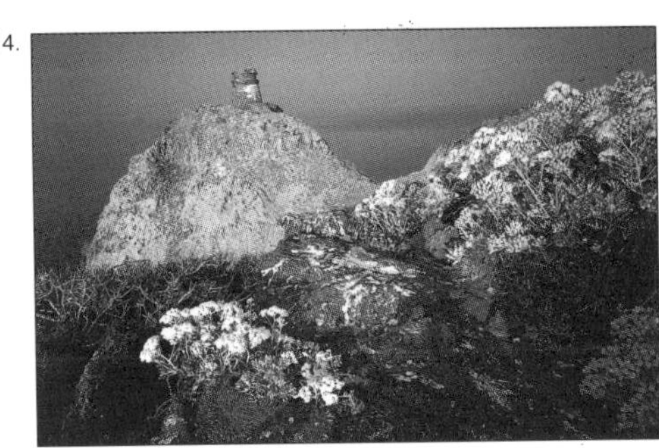

Cala Rossa, the Red Cove, and the island of Capraia, with the Zenòbito, its last active volcano. The cove is also home to one of the largest Tyrrhenian colonies of herring gulls.

15.

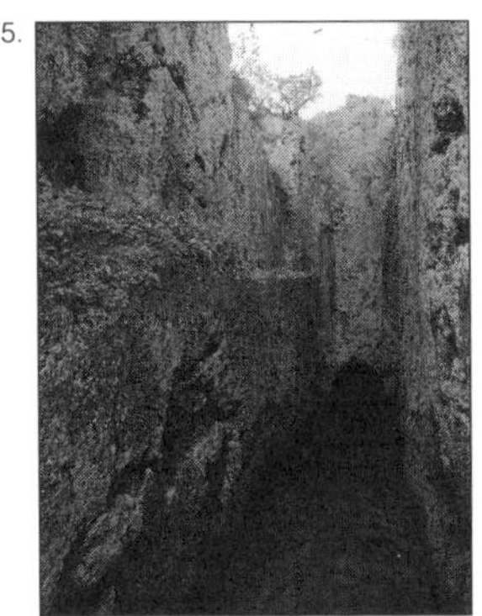

An ancient channel, partly exposed and partly underground, that once served the port of the Roman colony Cosa.

◀ 0 |45° |90° |135° |180° |200° |220° |240° |260°

16.

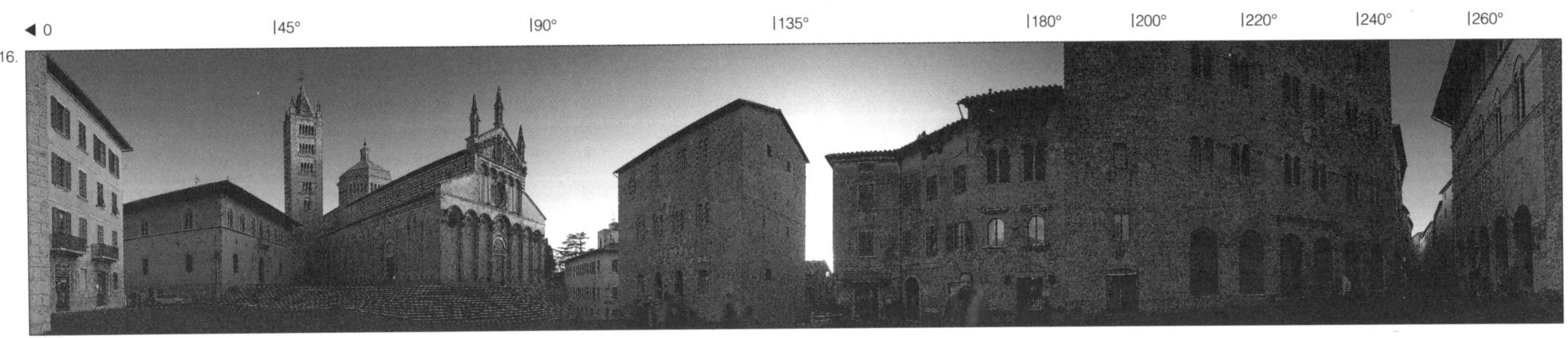

The Piazza Garibaldi, at Massa Marittima.

17.

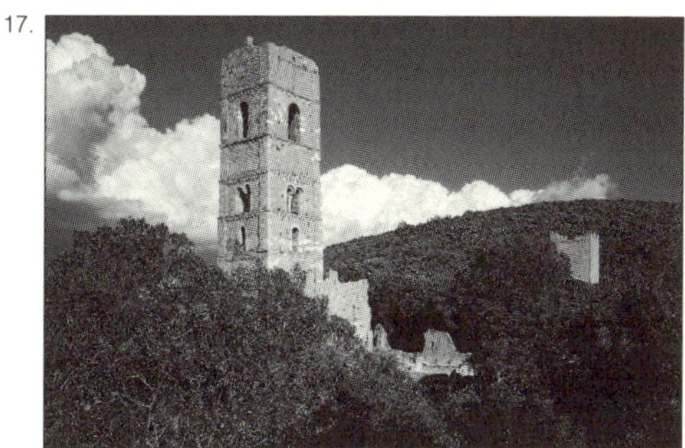

◀ 0 |45° |90° |135° |180°

18.

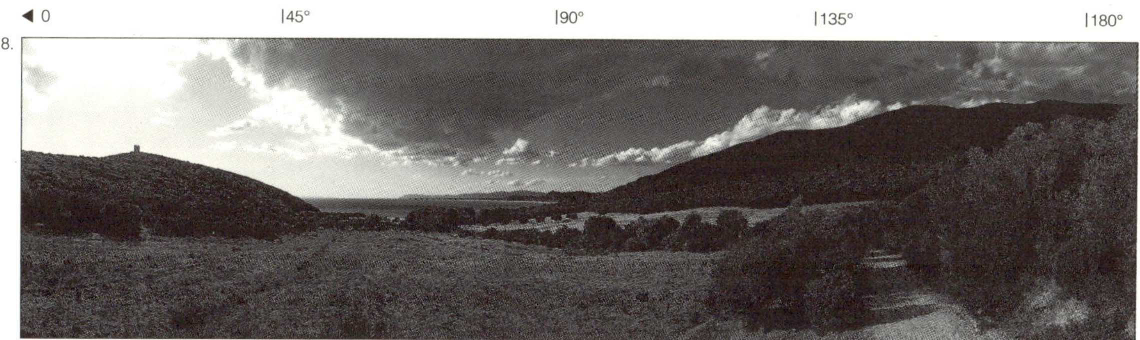

The Maremma natural park, 12.5 miles of undeveloped coastline at the mouth of the river Ombrone. Atop the Monti dell'Uccellina hills (left) is the abbey of San Rabano, accessible only by foot or on horseback.

◀ 0 |45° |90°

19.

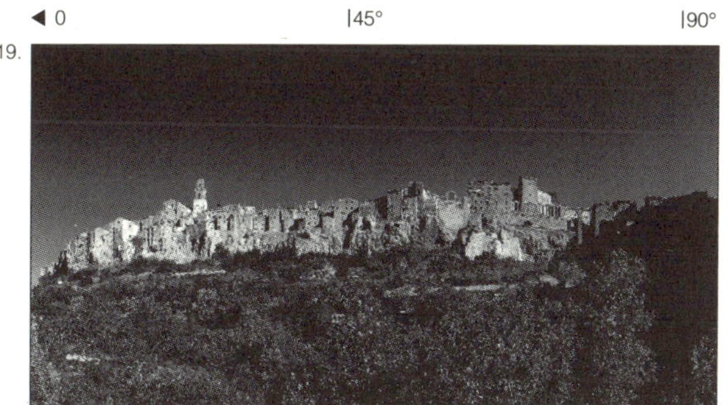

The town of Pitigliano, which dates back to ancient times.

◀ 0 |45° |90° |135°

20.

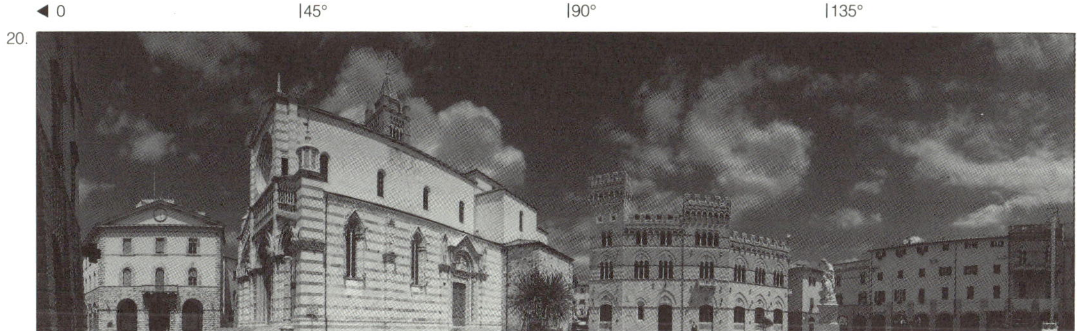

Piazza Duomo, Grosseto. From the left: the Palazzo Comunale, the Duomo (begun in 1294), the Palazzo della Provincia, and the Piazza Dante.

21.

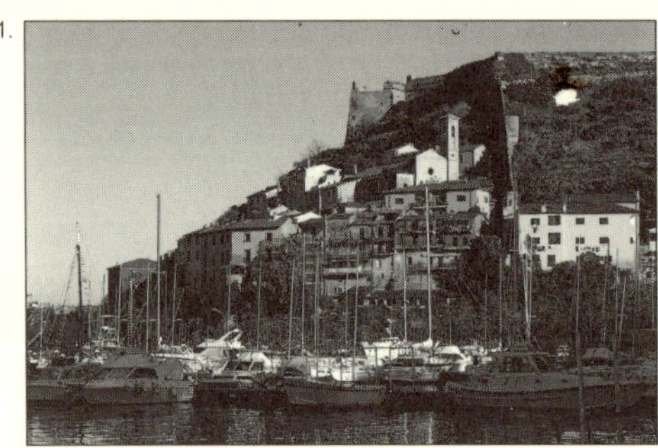

Port'Ercole, with the forts of Santa Barbara, Monte Filippo, and Stella; below them, the parish church where Caravaggio is interred.

22.

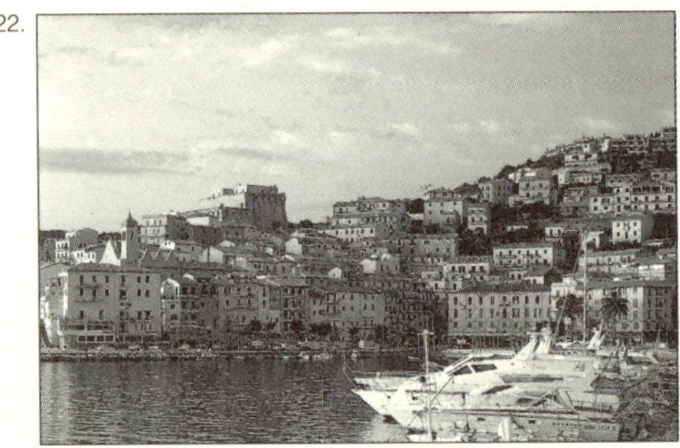

Porto Santo Stefano. The town suffered particular damage in the air raids of World War II and required extensive reconstruction afterward.

◀ 0 | 45° | 90° | 135°

23.

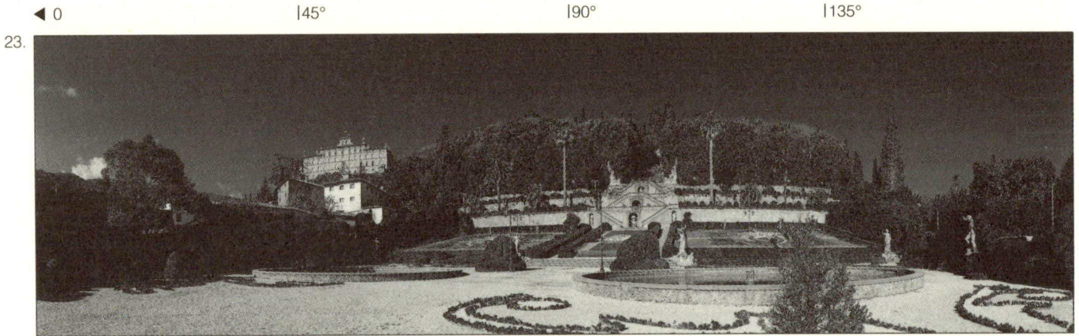

The gardens of the Parco di Villa Garzoni, in Collodi.

◀ 0 |45° |90° |135° |180° |200° |220° |240° |260°

24.

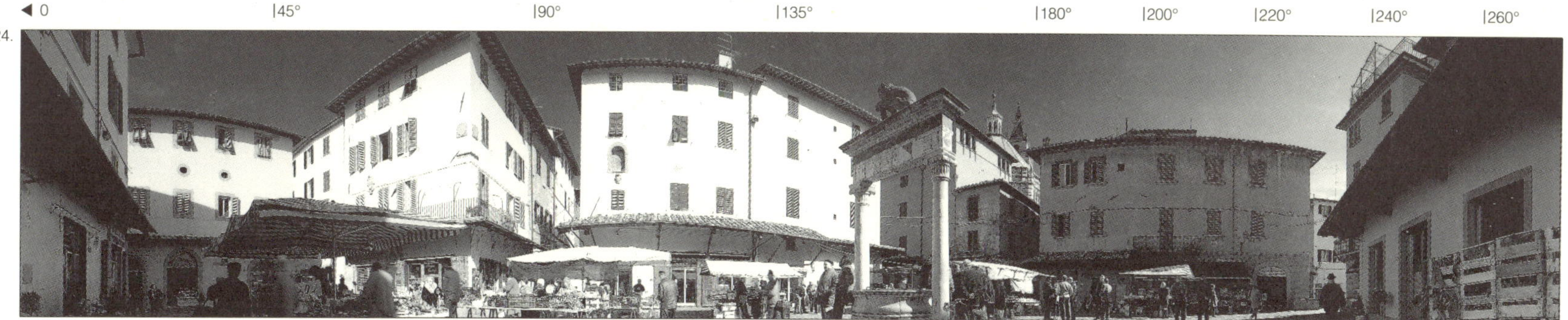

The piazza of Pistoia—known also as "la Sala" and as Piazza del Mercato. A well, il Pozzo del Leoncino, stands in its center.

◀ 0 |45° |90° |135° |180°

25.

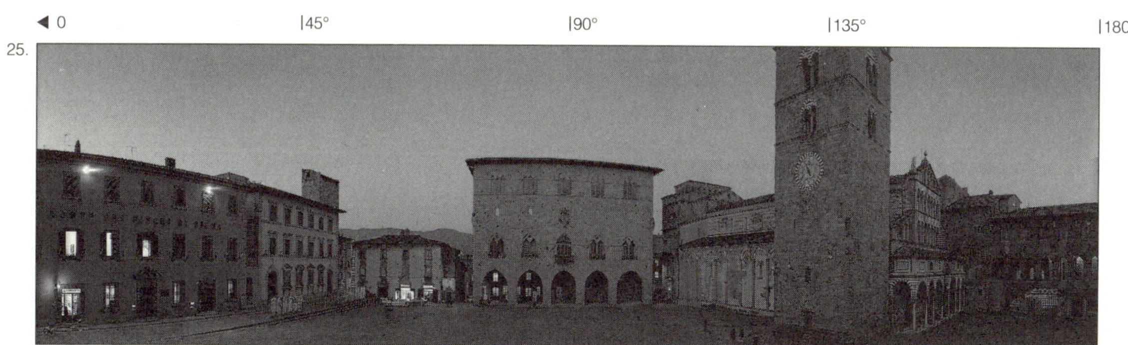

Pistoia's Piazza Duomo, with the Palazzo del Comune and the Palazzo del Podestà facing each other, and the Duomo.

26.

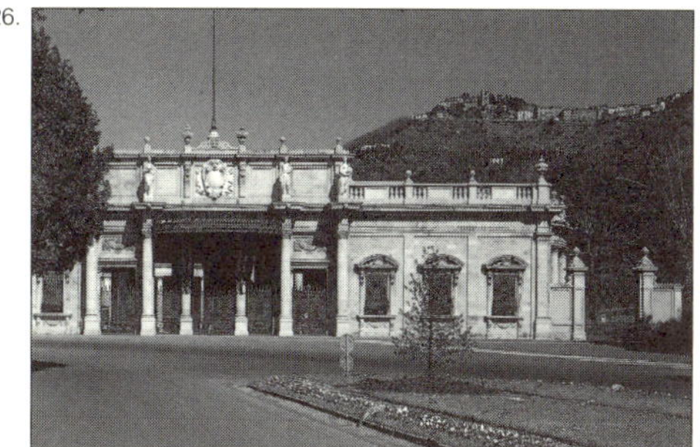

The Tettuccio spa, with the town of Montecatini in the background.

27.

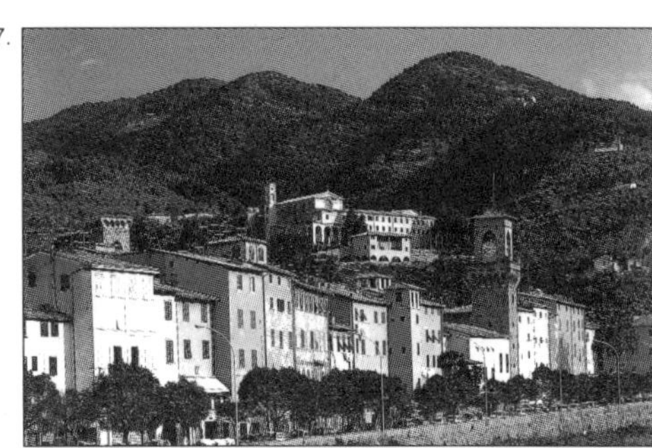

The riverfront of the city of Pescia, today an important center in the flower trade.

◀ 0 | 45° | 90° | 135° | 180°

28.

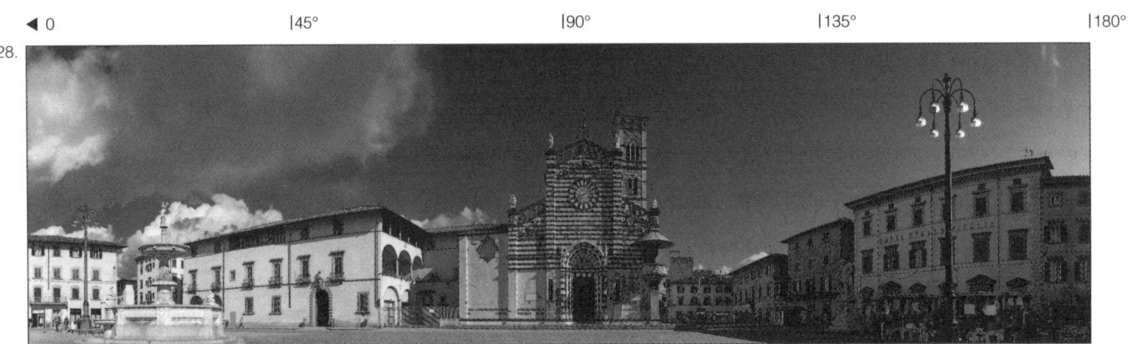

Piazza Duomo, Prato.

◀ 0 | 45° | 90° | 135° | 180° | 200° | 220° | 240° | 260° | 280°

29.

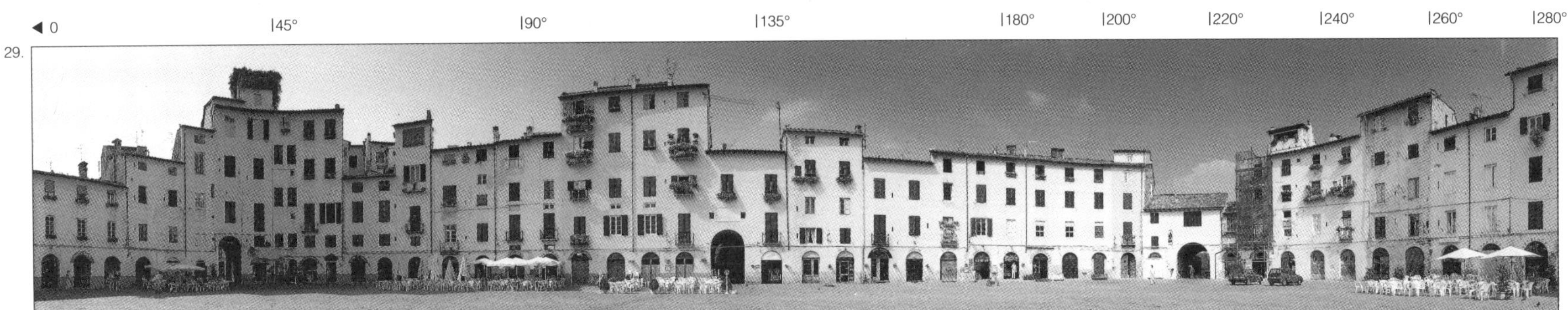

Piazza del Mercato, Lucca.

30.

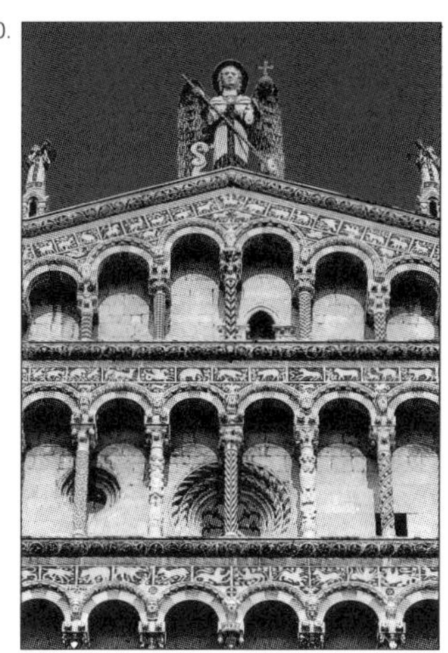

Detail of the façade of the church of San Michele.

31.

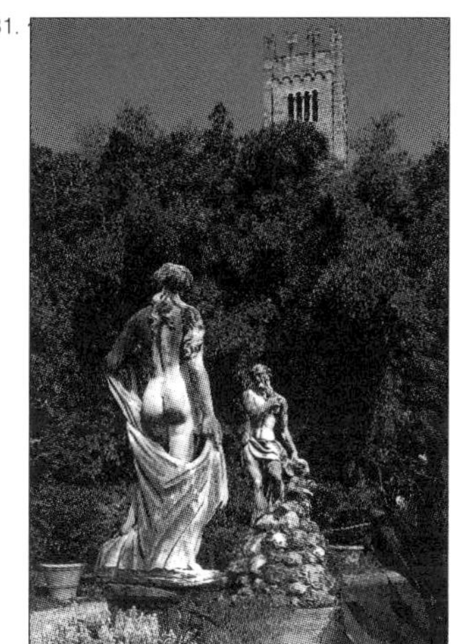

The Palazzo Pfanner gardens, established in the eighteenth century.

32.

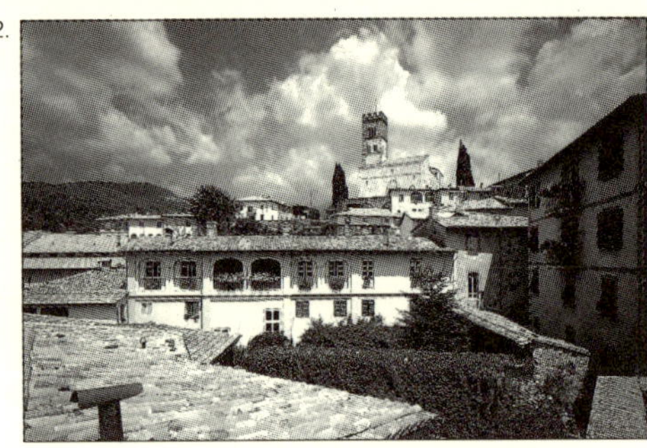

Barca, largely of medieval design, in the center of the Serchio Valley.

33.

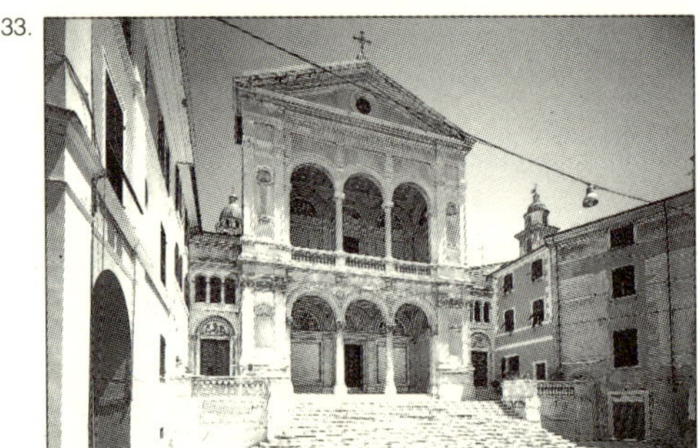

Duomo, Massa Cathedral.

34.

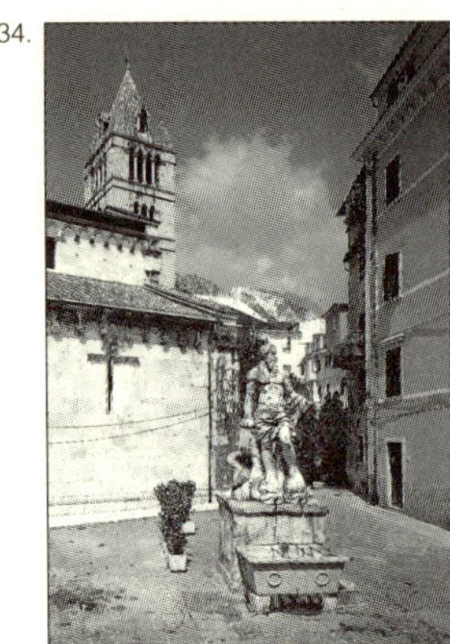

The Duomo of Carrara, neighboring town of Massa, with the Apuan Alps in the background.

35.

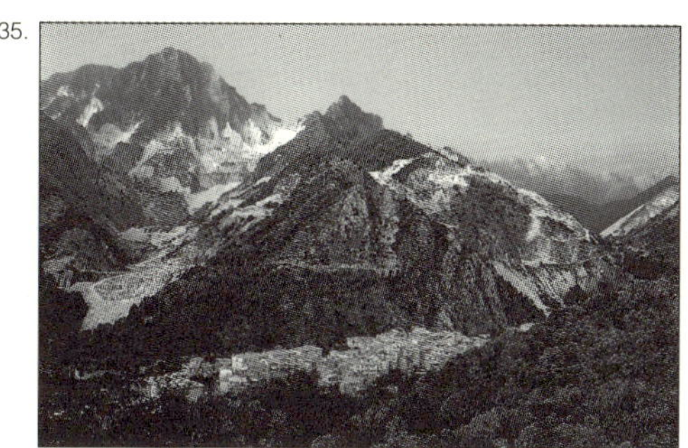

Bedizzano, a marble center for the past two thousand years.

36.

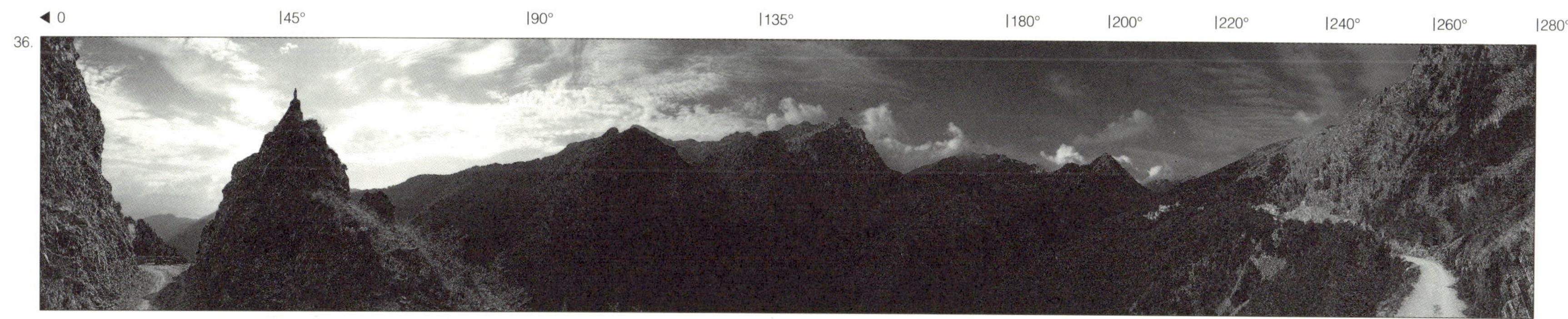

Mount Corchia, Pizzo delle Saette, Pania della Croce, and Pania Secca—some of the best-known peaks of the Apuans, a range with high-altitude plains, lush forests, and a vast underground network of caves.

37.

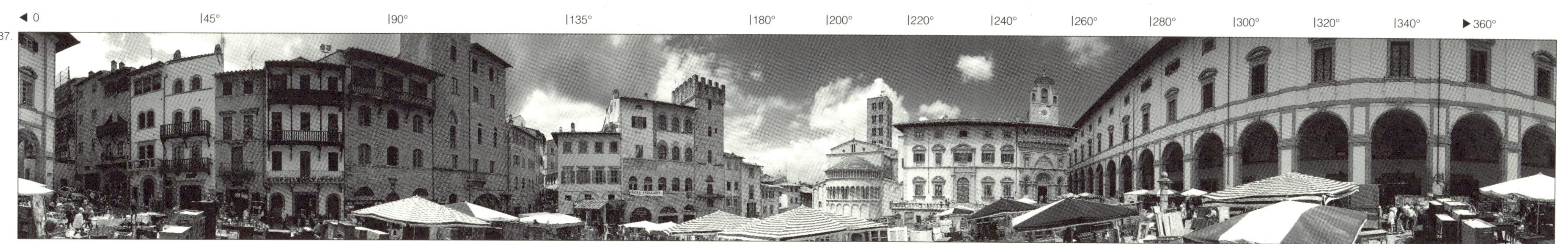

Arezzo's Piazza Grande: from the left, tall and narrow wooden-balconied medieval houses, the Palazzo del Tribunale (topped by its 1552 clock), and the Palazzo delle Logge.

38.

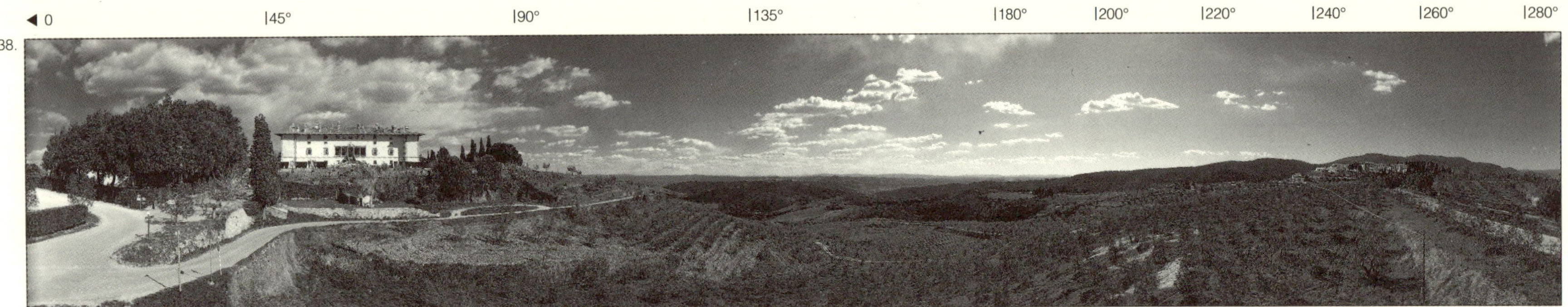

The Villa di Artimino, the favorite Medicean country residence.

39.

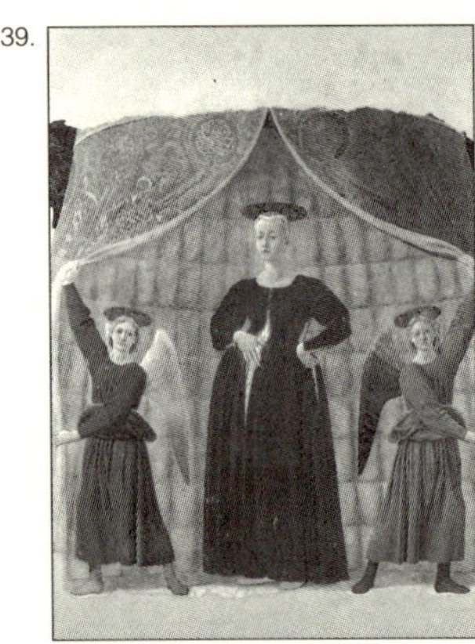

The Madonna del Parto in Monterchi, by Piero Della Francesca. Even today, expectant mothers come to view this painting and pray for an untroubled pregnancy.

40.

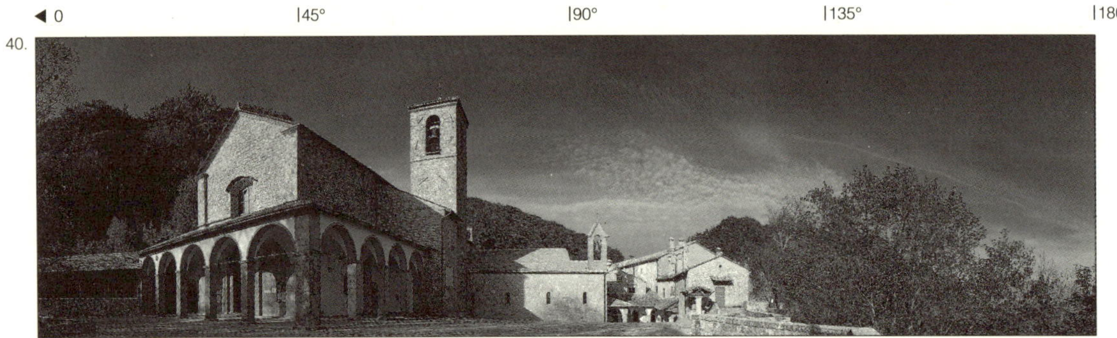

Franciscan sanctuary, La Verna.

41

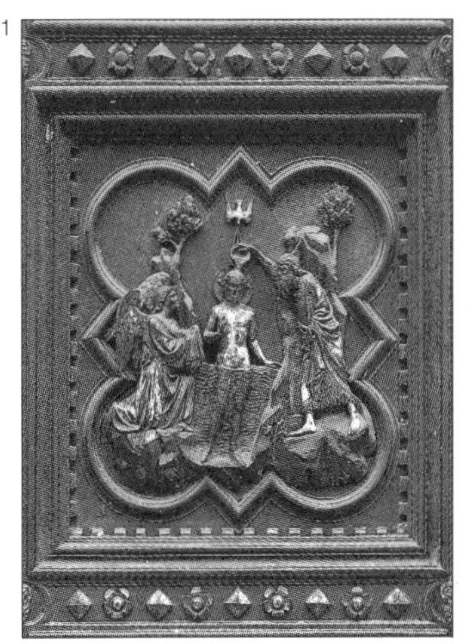

Florence: the Baptistery's gilded bronze south door, by Andrea Pisano, showing the baptism of Christ.

42.

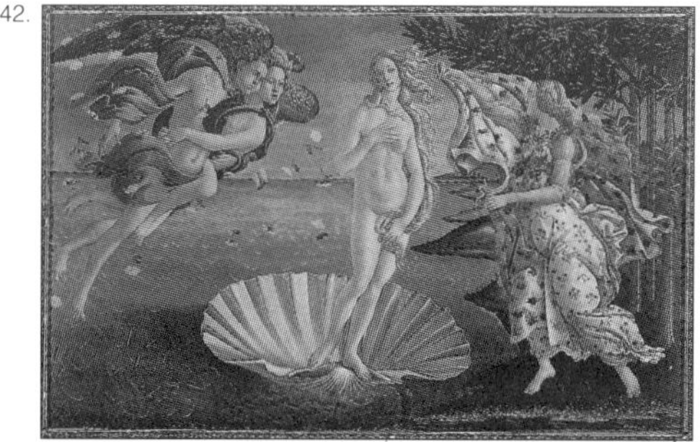

The Birth of Venus, by Botticelli, in the Uffizi.

43.

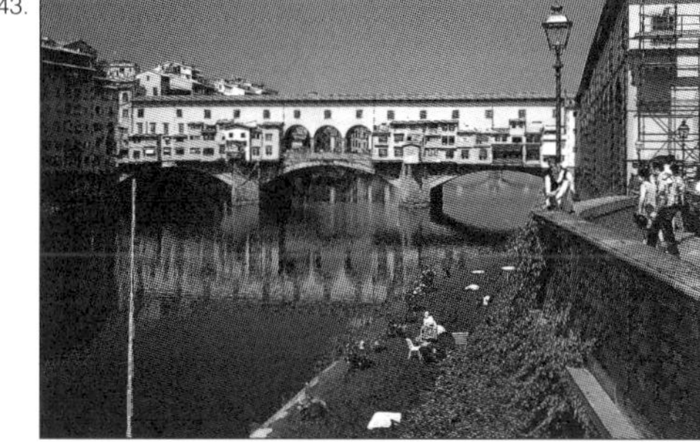

Florence's Ponte Vecchio, a bridge that dates back to at least 996.

44.

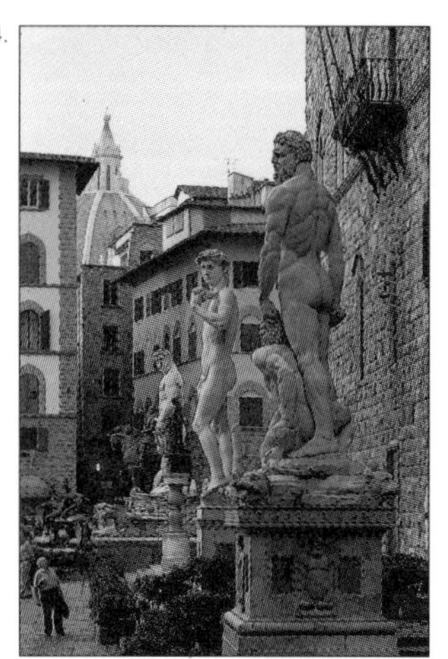

The Palazzo Vecchio of Florence, with some of its many sculptures: Hercules and Cacus, Michelangelo's David (a copy), Judith and Holofernes by Donatello (also a copy), the fountain of Neptune, and the equestrian statue of Cosimo I. In the background, Via de' Cerchi and the Duomo.

45.

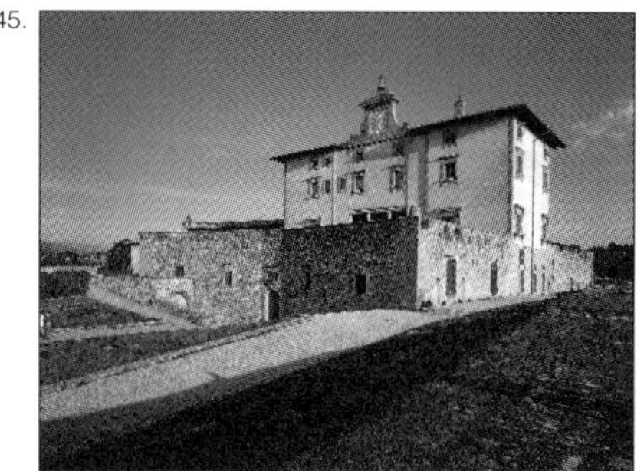

The Forte di San Giorgio, or Forte Belvedere, in Florence.

◀ 0 |45° |90° |135°

46.

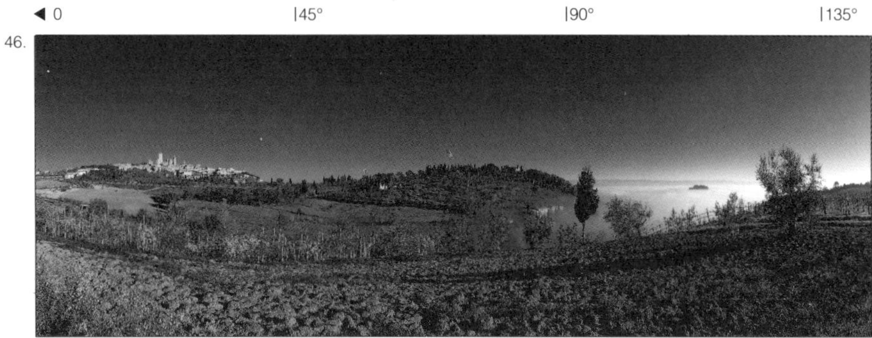

Countryside around San Gimignano, once a leading producer and exporter of saffron.

47.

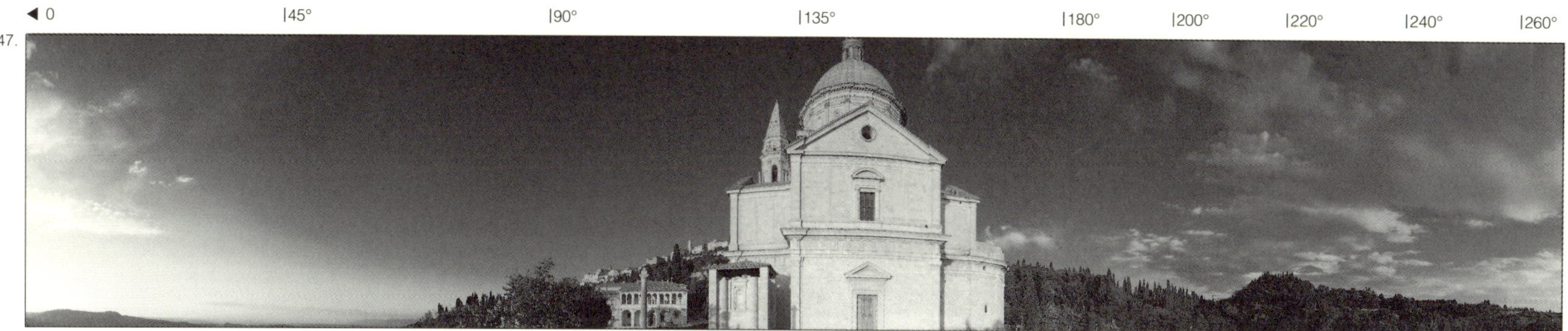

The Church of St. Blaise, designed by Antonio da Sangallo the Elder.

48.

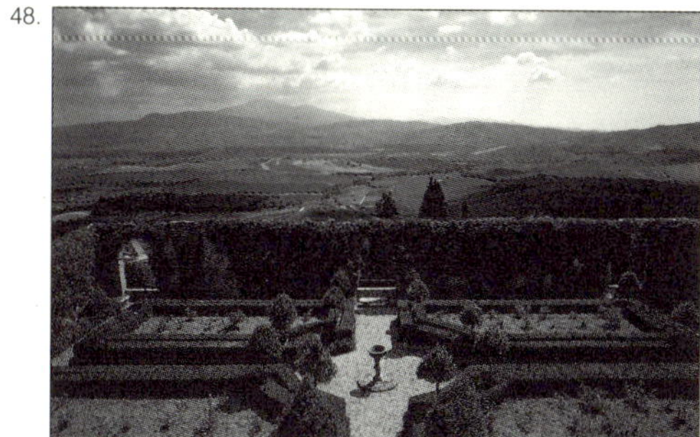

Pienza: the gardens of Palazzo Piccolòmini with Mount Amiata in the background. Pienza was essentially established by Enea Silvio Piccolòmini (Pope Pius II) in the fifteenth century, transforming what had been Corsignano. The Palazzo di Famiglia, shown here, has a square design, with a courtyard and a hanging garden.

49.

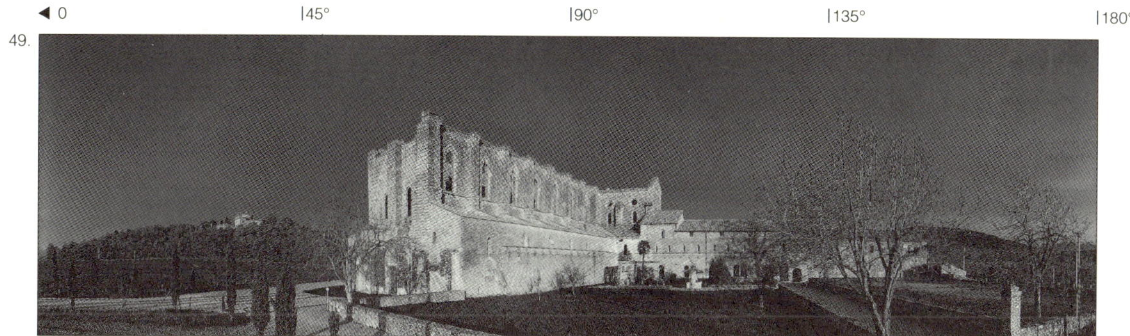

The legendary abbey San Galgano, formerly one of the most important Cistercian abbeys in Italy. It was used as a farm in the nineteenth century, and today it houses a small drug-rehabilitation community.

50.

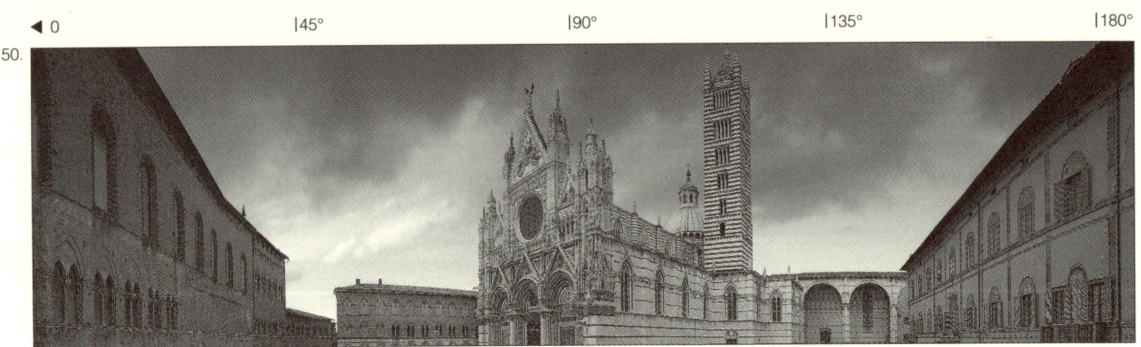

Siena's Piazza del Duomo. Its dome, completed in 1264, is one of the oldest in Italy.

51.

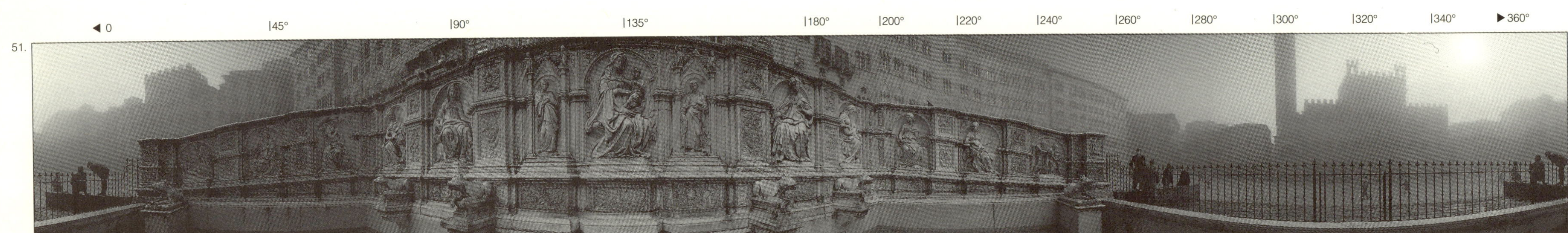

Piazza del Campo has been an essential Siena site since the early Middle Ages, when it was simply a large clearing outside of town where markets were held.

52.

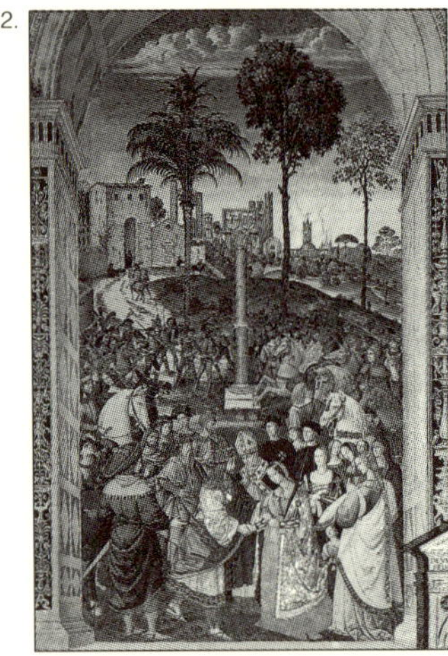

From a series of frescoes by Bernardino di Betto—known as "Il Pinturicchio"—commissioned by Cardinal Francesco Todeschini Piccolòmini in 1502. This scene shows the meeting of Federico III and his betrothed, Eleanor of Portugal.

53.

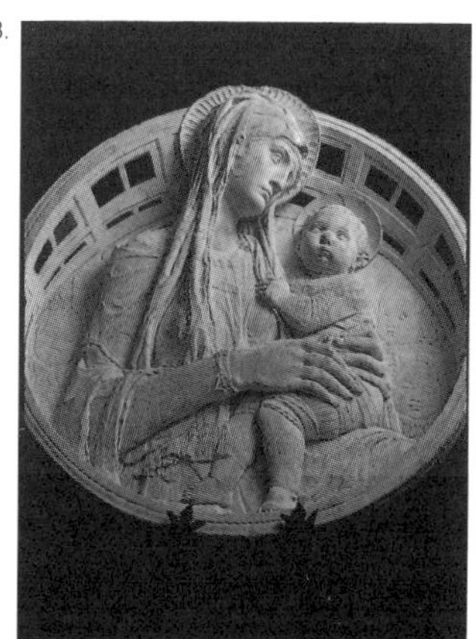

Madonna and Child (1457), marble, by Donatello, in the Museo dell'Opera Metropolitana.

54.

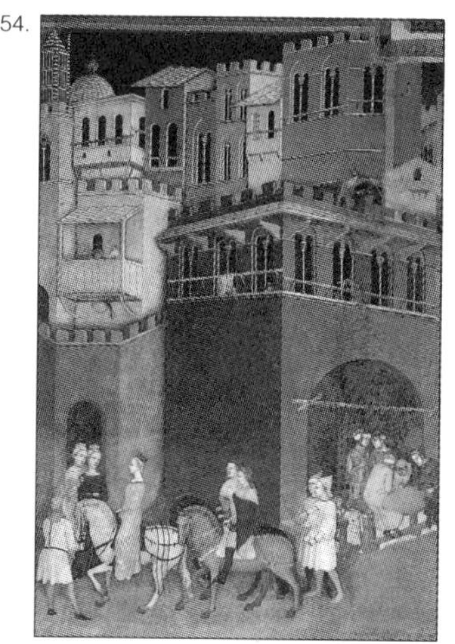

A fresco by Ambrogio Lorenzetti, in the Palazzo Pubblico, Siena. From the first and largest secular pictorial cycle of the Middle Ages, produced by Lorenzetti between 1337 and 1339.

◀ 0 | 45° | 90° | 135°

55.

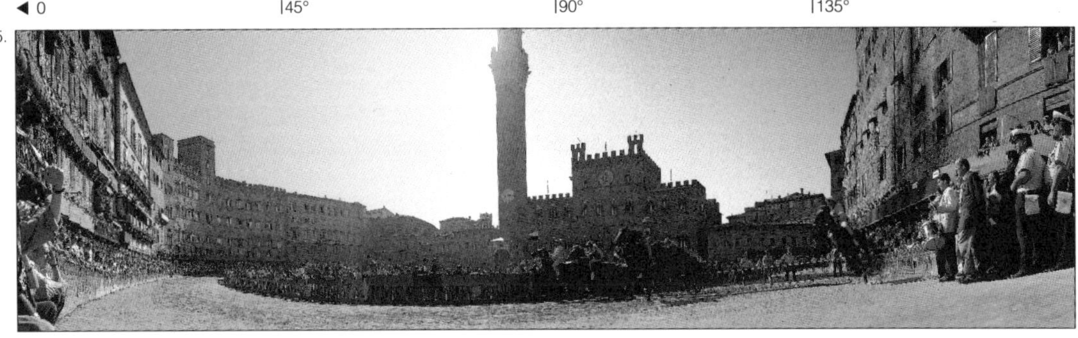

In Siena, rehearsals for the Palio—an elaborate, citywide festival of races, held twice a year, that dates back to at least the sixteenth century and now takes place in the Campo.

56.

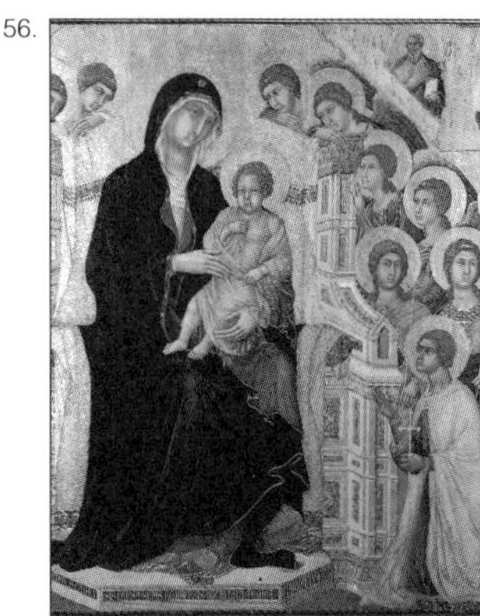

La Maestà, by Duccio di Boninsegna, in the Museo dell'Opera Metropolitana, Siena. This is the artist's masterpiece, and one of the largest existing Italian paintings.

53.

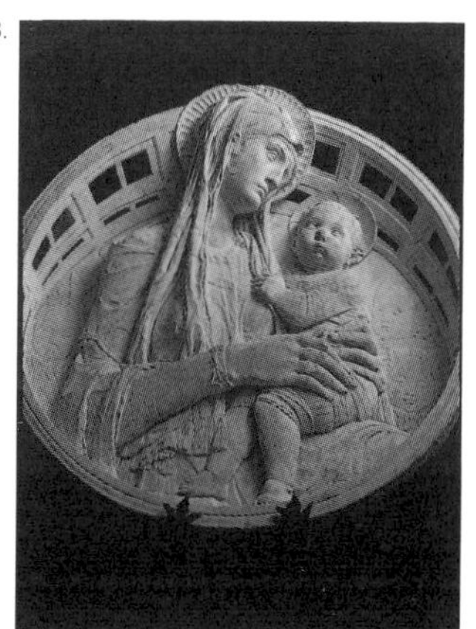

Madonna and Child (1457), marble, by Donatello, in the Museo dell'Opera Metropolitana.

54.

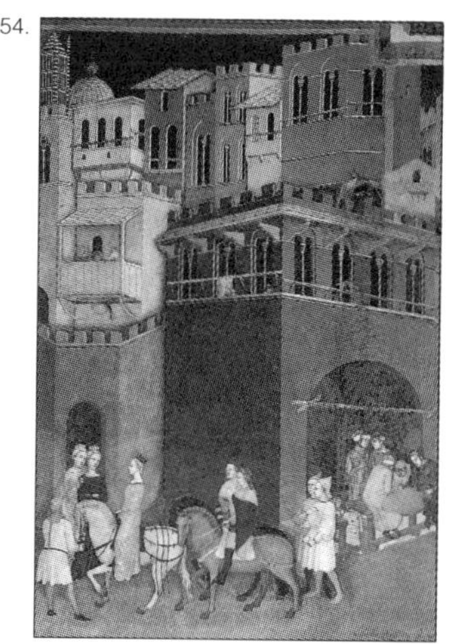

A fresco by Ambrogio Lorenzetti, in the Palazzo Pubblico, Siena. From the first and largest secular pictorial cycle of the Middle Ages, produced by Lorenzetti between 1337 and 1339.

55.

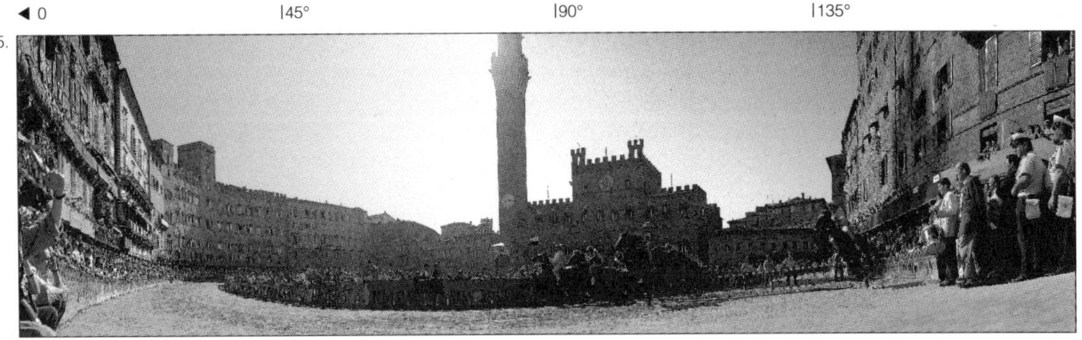

In Siena, rehearsals for the Palio—an elaborate, citywide festival of races, held twice a year, that dates back to at least the sixteenth century and now takes place in the Campo.

56.

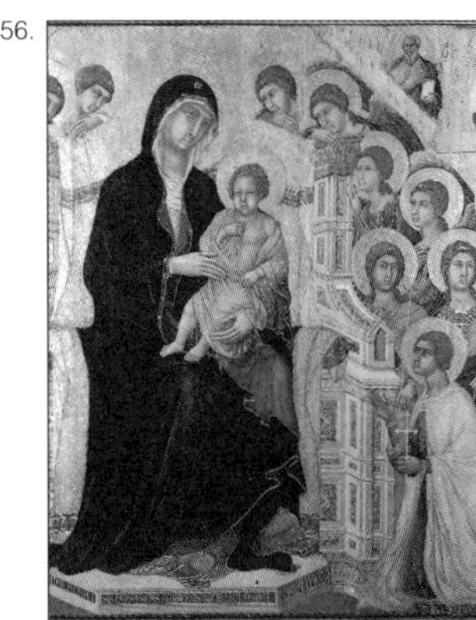

La Maestà, by Duccio di Boninsegna, in the Museo dell'Opera Metropolitana, Siena. This is the artist's masterpiece, and one of the largest existing Italian paintings.